Enthusiastic

"A most interesting new book that helps us let go of our fight against God."
   Gerald G. Jampolsky, M.D.
   Author, *Love Is Letting Go of Fear*

". . . an impelling book by a gifted clinician who clearly matches the courage of her patients with her own. I recommend *Rage at God*, not only to therapists but also to all who long for guidance to that bottom rung of the ladder to ascension."
   Terry Santino, A.T.R.

"Truly an inspired and an inspiring work—a must for those whose quest is wholeness, completion."
   Rev. J. Michael Ferguson

"Anneliese Widman takes readers right into the consultation room with three of her clients, revealing in graphic detail how . . . she helps unconsciously tortured and torturing human beings find more healthful, hopeful, loving lives and relationships. Therapists, clients, and the curious public will be interested and well informed."
   E. J. Svasta, Jr., M.S.W.
   Faculty, International Institute for Bioenergetic Analysis

"Dazzling portrayals from the cutting edge of a therapeutic modality that integrates Psyche, Soma, and Spiritual Growth."
   Eva Shelby, M.S.W.
   Certified Past-Life Therapist

Rage at God

Anneliese Widman, Ph.D.

Also by Anneliese Widman, Ph.D.

MY FEMALE, MY MALE, MY SELF, AND GOD:
A Modern Woman in Search of Her Soul

Rage at God

Ascending to Reunion

Anneliese Widman, Ph.D.

ANT HILL PRESS
GEORGETOWN, MASSACHUSETTS

Copyright © 1998
Anneliese Widman, Ph.D.

ISBN: 0-9655067-2-X

First printing: April 1998

All rights reserved. No part of this book may be reproduced by any means or in any form whatsoever without written permission from the publisher, except for brief quotations embodied in literary articles or reviews. For permissions and reprint information, contact the publisher.

Ant Hill Press
P. O. Box 10
Georgetown, MA 01833
(978) 352-9976 • fax (978) 352-5586
http://www.ReadersNdex.com/northstar

Cover Design: Salwen Studios, Keene, NH
Cover Art: Deborah Freedman

Printed in Canada

The author gratefully acknowledges permission to use material from *The Other Bible* by Willis Barnstone, Editor. Copyright © 1984 by Willis Barnstone. Used by permission of Bantam Books, a division of Bantam Doubleday Dell Publishing Group, Inc.

Publisher's Cataloging-in-Publication

Widman, Anneliese.
    Rage at God : ascending to reunion / Anneliese Widman.
  — 1st ed.
    p. cm.
    ISBN: 0-9655067-2-X

    1. Bioenergetic psychotherapy—Case studies. 2. Anger—Religious aspects. 3. Mind and body therapies. I. Title

RC489.B5W54 1998   616.89'14
                              QBI98-615

To the Monday Night Group:
Arthur, Bill, Bronwen, Bruce,
Carol, Cate, Deborah,
Douglas, Graham, Grazia, Joan,
Kathe, Larry, Luis, Lynn, Mark,
Martha, Michael, Tootsie—
*who are courageously conquering
their rage at God and ascending.*

"... I saw a brazen ladder of wondrous length reaching up to heaven, but so narrow that only one could ascend at once; and on the sides of the ladder were fastened all kinds of iron weapons. There were swords, lances, hooks, daggers, so that if anyone went up carelessly or without looking upwards he was mangled and his flesh caught on the weapons. And just beneath the ladder was a dragon couching of wondrous size who lay in wait for those going up and sought to frighten them from going up. . . . and as though I were treading on the first step, I trod on his head. And I went up, and saw a vast expanse of garden, and in the midst a man sitting with white hair, in the dress of a shepherd, a tall man, milking sheep; and round about were many thousands clad in white. And he raised his head, and looked upon me, and said: 'You have well come, my child.' And he called me, and gave me a morsel of the milk which he was milking and I received it in my joined hands, and ate; and all they that stood around said: 'Amen.'"

The Passion of Perpetua and Felicity
(from *The Other Bible*, Willis Barnstone, Editor)

Contents

Foreword ix
Preface xi
The Soul of Man xv

Part One—Marda

1. The Soul of Marda 3
2. Our First Encounter 11
3. Explaining the Modality 15
4. Marda's Environment 19
5. Marda's Impressions 23
6. Marda Was a Challenge 25
7. The Next Session 31
8. What a Dream! 37
9. Reflectivism: The Female Energy 47
10. Marda and the Group 57
11. Reflectivism: The Male Energy 61
12. Marda's Wake-up Call 71
13. The Initial Layer 75
14. Marda's Resolve 81

Part Two—Christopher

15. The Soul of Christopher 85
16. Our First Encounter 91
17. The Next Session—Robbed of Life 95
18. The Next Time 99

19.	Margaret—Ambivalence	105
20.	Victimization	111
21.	Victimization versus Reflectivism	117
22.	Reflectivism: The Male Energy	121
23.	Reflectivism: The Female Energy	129
24.	The Missing Piece	137
25.	Fulfillment	143

Part Three—Didi

26.	The Soul of Didi	149
27.	The First Session with Didi	155
28.	Didi's Father and the Men in Her Life	161
29.	Didi's Mother	167
30.	Didi's Female and Male Energies	171
31.	Alan	177
32.	Didi's Introduction to the Group	181
33.	Two of Didi's Past Lives	189
34.	Another Life with a Pinch of Arrogance	207

Guide to Terms Used in this Book 217

Foreword

I find it hard to contain my admiration for Anneliese Widman's bravery and resolution in helping the life-scarred heal themselves. Bravery, because every cultural taboo enlists to repress the very concept of "rage at God." Resolution, because in *Rage at God* she demonstrates that the therapeutic modalities she has developed—unorthodox as some may be—can in fact promote this healing of the soul. Now, through this book, she offers the benefit of her years of work to many more than she can personally counsel in her New York City practice.

As the title forces one to confront, *Rage at God* contains powerful, disturbing material, presented with unprecedented frankness. The upheaval in our comfortable cultural shibboleths is the source of the value, both unique and timely, of this work. Something is very wrong with the ordering of our society—indeed, of our world—Anneliese Widman is saying, and that wrong thing is our obstinate denial of unpalatable truths about ourselves.

In answer to the problems she poses, Widman offers her stunning concept of *Reflectivism*—reminding us of what we seem to wish to forget, that in self-responsibility lies the only possible meaning of life. From this follows inevitably her acute intuition that egocentric division of original Unity derived, continues to derive, from—rage at God. Original Sin has been defined in words a bright ten-year-old can understand.

It will be in proceeding from that understanding that all peace of heart and joy in existence with God is reclaimed. For her part in helping others along our common journey, I felicitate Anneliese Widman.

Alcott Allison
Author, *The White Stone*

Preface

I am a Bioenergetic psychotherapist in practice for over twenty years, who has moved beyond the traditional forms of psychoanalysis. I am interested in seeing the patient grow from the "I" state of consciousness to the "I am" state of consciousness. The categories and concepts that will be addressed in this book—notably, Reflectivism, my theory of a soul's prenatal choice of characterized parents to illustrate to the soul its own need of specific rectification—were elucidated in my first book, *My Female, My Male, My Self, and God: A Modern Woman in Search of Her Soul*.

Other concepts will be introduced as the reader journeys with the three patients whose process of discovery and growth have been explored in this book. All three patients have arrived at an "I" consciousness and are groping for an "I am" consciousness. All are striving to overcome their destiny, not only in this life but also from lives of the past. I hope a learning process about the path to ascension will become evident to the reader.

It is my belief that we are all riddled with a subconscious rage, noticeable from the moment of conception to the time the organism emerges from the womb into life. This rage is at God, for casting us out of heaven. While in heaven we wanted to grow, but we never wanted the responsibility of what growth entails. Therefore we rage at the Essence from which we have sprung for throwing us into the tumult of earthly experiences. We rage and we rage, remaining unreconciled to our descent, bringing to ourselves sins of the worst kind. Eons of time, eons of living, centuries pass before the soul screams: "Enough of this! I'm taking over!"

Rage is a powerful energy. It is a force that can obliterate all other realities. It is a force, that, if used indiscriminately and unconsciously, will in time obliterate the perceptive capacity of the human being. It blocks out acumen and judgment and dominates all other feelings, placing the human being into a state of driven unconsciousness.

The groundwork of psychology, scientifically established for the last one hundred years, has proved of great advantage to the human psyche. It is now time for the boundaries of psychology to be stretched to include other wisdoms, other insights, additional higher understanding about the human being. If the psychological modality will not expand its boundaries to include reincarnation, karma, and past lives, it will stay hopelessly enmeshed in redundancy. People will remain fixated on blaming their parents instead of taking responsibility for their own lives, as they will be able to do more readily when they incorporate concepts such as *Reflectivism*, and the female and male energies, in their being.

I should like to propose the following image:

> God's firmament is filled with souls,
> but the ascending souls,
> clear about
> their motivation to return,
> clear about
> their love for God,
> and
> having cleansed themselves of their hatred,
> having joined their female with their male,
> will now join the universe
> as enlightened
> souls.
> As enlightened souls,
> they will be
> incorporated into God's host of
> angels,

souls
who will become helpers to those
ascending the ladder,
the ladder leading from
darkness,
into the light.

Anneliese Widman, Ph.D.
March 1998

The Soul of Man

The care which God exercised in fashioning every detail of the body of man is as naught in comparison with his solicitude for the human soul. . . . it is the spirit of God moving upon the face of the waters.

. . . When a woman has conceived, the Angel of the Night, Lailah, carries the sperm before God, and God decrees what manner of human being shall become of it. . . . Piety and wickedness alone are left to the determination of man himself. Then God makes a sign to the angel appointed over the souls, saying, "Bring me the soul so-and-so, which is hidden in Paradise. . . ." The angel brings the designated soul, and she bows down when she appears in the presence of God, and prostrates herself before him. At that moment, God issues the command, "Enter this sperm." The soul opens her mouth, and pleads: "O Lord of the world! I am well pleased with the world in which I have been living since the day on which you called me into being. Why do you now desire to have me enter this impure sperm, I who am holy and pure, and a part of your glory?" God consoles her: "The world which I shall cause you to enter is better than the world in which you have lived hitherto, and when I created you, it was only for this purpose." The soul is then forced to enter the sperm against her will, and the angel carries her back to the womb of the mother. Two angels are detailed to watch that she shall not leave it, nor drop out of it, and a light is set above her, whereby the soul can see from one end of the world to the other. In the morning an angel carries her to Paradise, and shows her the righteous, who sit there in their glory, with crowns upon their heads. . . .

In the evening, the angel takes the soul to Hell, and there points out the sinners whom the angels of destruction are smiting with fiery scourges, the sinners all the while crying out, "Woe! Woe!" but no mercy is shown unto them. . . .

Between morning and evening the angel carries the soul around, and shows her where she will live and where she will die, and the place where she will be buried, and he takes her through the whole world, and points out the just and the sinners and all things. In the evening, he replaces her in the womb of the mother, and there she remains for nine months.

When the time arrives for her to emerge from the womb into the open world, the same angel addresses the soul, "The time has come for you to go abroad into the open world." The soul demurs, "Why do you want to make me go forth into the open world?" The angel replies: "Know that as you were formed against your will, so now you will be born against your will, and against your will you shall die, and against your will you shall give account of yourself before the King of kings, the Holy One, blessed be he." But the soul is reluctant to leave her place. Then the angel fillips the babe on the nose, extinguishes the light at his head, and brings him forth into the world against his will. Immediately the child forgets all his soul has seen and learnt, and he comes into the world crying, for he loses a place of shelter and security and rest. (The Haggadah, from *The Other Bible*, Willis Barnstone, Editor)

Part One

Marda

1

The Soul of Marda

*I am here, there, and everywhere;
Not down there, thank God.
Safe,
in my beehive compartment,
Safe—from him,
standing, a celestial watchman—
silvery net in hand.
Net suspended from a long, long pole
to catch recalcitrant souls.*

*Such as I?
Huh!
He doesn't dare.
I'll destroy the firmament
sooner than be taken.*

*Oh, hush, you singing angels.
I don't want to hear, to see,
to feel.
My eyes are slits—
I see you, but I really don't.*

You're in the mist.
Shadows that can't come
near.
Stay away—all.
Especially you, God.
Do You hear?

As for you, Angel of Destiny,
silly, prideful soul,
monstrous executioner,
who gives me naught but dread.
You submit spinelessly to God.
But what will that get you?
A reprieve from going
to that hellish place?
Not so, goody-goodness.
You'll go down there like
the rest of us.

Should they send me down,
I'll be so far removed
from whatever resembles
humanness.

A "golem" I'll become—
stiff, half dead,
buried alive inside.
I'll scheme and plot,
look at all through my
slitted eyes—
organs impossible to read.

I've got my disguise.
Now I feel safe

*from the pressures
of this heaven.
I'll sleep and dream.
No one dares come near.*

*Oh dreams,
you are welcome
in this demanding heaven.
Let go! Surrender!
Ah! there it is—
Ecstasy!*

*God loves me, after all.
I'm close to God—
cradled in His arms.
He rocks me tenderly.
Is it a lullaby I hear?
Oh, Lord!
We'll be like this
forever.*

*The others are envious.
But, never mind—
I'm getting what I want.
I won't open my eyes.
It would be useless.
The mist is too thick;
I see only what I want to see.*

*I smile as I dream,
a baby-contented smile.
I gurgle and gooh-gah
vocally.
Until I notice the Angel of*

*Destiny standing by my side,
his silvery net strategically placed,
waiting to pull me
into it.*

*My golem nature
emerges menacingly.
I neither hear, see, nor feel.
The angel, undaunted,
pushes me forward:
"It's time to go down.
You've slumbered enough.
Go down and rectify.
Strive for your angelic state."*

*The angel continues to push
me on.
I'm stiff, unreachable.
Though on my feet,
I barely move.
But he insists.*

*We inch our way to the
karmic Council.
I grunt, golem-like,
refusing to speak.
We arrive at the Council's
portals.*

*"What have we here?"
they ask, looking at me
quizzically.
"Are you ailing, soul of God?
Speak, tell us your desires."*

MARDA

"Mmmmm, mmmmmmm," was
my only response,
so buried was I inside my shell.
"Mmmmm, mmmmmmm."

They listen, perplexed.
"You desire to return,
we surmise.
We are glad and we
give you a female body.
Let your life be productive
and real."

"NO! NO! NO!" I shout,
my golem persona
broken into pieces.
"NO! NO! NO!
How dare you make me do
what I don't want?"

"I'll never be alive—
I'll never be a woman.
I'll never grow up.
I want only to be nurtured
by God."

"Dearest soul,
you must learn to separate,
to become one with yourself.
Find your wholeness within.
Return then to our heaven,
in a state of completion.
Grow into the angel you
really are."

*I become the golem more
intensely than ever.
They could not budge me
from the spot.*

*"Mmmmmmm,"
was the only sound
that emerged from me,
as the angel carried me to
the landing depot.*

*There he placed me into
his net,
where I lay like a statue.
We glided slowly down to Earth—
to where two people
were copulating.*

*The woman lay,
her legs apart—
the man, dazed—
propelled by her desire,
had mounted her.
"This is the thing to do,"
he thought.
"It will be over soon."*

*"I've got him now,"
the woman gloated inside
herself.
"He's a handsome catch
at my time of life."*

MARDA

*The angel pulled me out
of his net.
I uttered a heart-rending
mumble
as he introduced me into the
woman's womb.
I was as stiff and numb
as the man on top,
while the woman grabbed
whatever warmth he gave her.*

*"Oh, God," I thought,
"How will I be nurtured
by a mummified man
and a woman whose neediness
strangles?"*

*A difficult soul?
Ah, yes.
But . . .*

*I'll foretell—
The soul did reach
the first
rung
of the
ladder.*

2

Our First Encounter

Marda is now forty years old. When I first met her, she was twenty-eight. She is a tall, strikingly beautiful blond woman who, when aware of being observed, seems to retreat into invisibility. When she came into my waiting room, she sat inconspicuously in the darkest corner. I went to her with extended hand. She stood up to take my hand, but her arm was rigid, keeping me at a noticeable distance.

I took her into my office. She stood like a statue in the middle of the room, gyrating slowly on her own axis, like a weather vane, not clear about her next direction.

I asked her to remove her coat. She shook her head quietly but firmly, placing her hands in her pockets, bringing her coat even closer to her body. She seemed like a being who had only just arrived on Earth and did not want to be here.

I encouraged her to sit in a chair opposite mine. She did so, her head lowered. The silence between us was intimidating. I did not quite know what to do next. Marda suddenly took her hands out of her pockets, stood up, faced me directly, and exclaimed loudly, "I don't know what I'm doing here. I'm here only because . . . because . . . ."

She did not finish her sentence, but sat down again, lowered her head. Her silence was stony, making my insides feel tight and breathless. It was as though her soul had died somewhere between her words and her actions.

"Were you born in New York?" I asked, hoping this question would stimulate some reaction.

"No," she answered, sinking her head into the lapels of her coat. "I'm from California. I left Berkeley after my sophomore year. I followed a friend to her hometown in Vermont. I stayed with her for two years, worked, saved some money—enough to return to California to finish my education. I have a B.A.—English literature. I want to write, be a playwright." She looked at me defiantly, as though I would challenge her ambition.

When I did not, she inclined her head and sucked the corner of one of the lapels of her coat like a nursing infant. The room became deathly silent.

"Who referred you to me?" I asked.

"The woman I lived with in Vermont. She'd heard about you from someone else. She suggested I do some therapy. Wouldn't tell me why, but because I trust her and like her, and since I'm living in New York now, I thought I would give it a try.

"I also had some group therapy as a teenager, but I don't remember any of it. All I can remember is that my schoolmates asked me why I was always frowning and why didn't I finish my sentences. The rest is buried inside me somewhere. I'm still frowning and not finishing my sentences, as you can see."

She looked at me with sparkling blue eyes that took me in, doing so in a full sweep. The eyes instantaneously became slits. The transformation astonished me. Once again she returned her head to her lapel.

"Are your parents alive?"

"They're alive. That is, one of them is; the other, just barely," she responded with wry amusement.

She rose, paced the room, her hands rubbing against each other. She was racked with anxiety. She circled the room, skirting around chairs, my desk, me, never ceasing to rub her hands. She made two circles around the various objects, then resumed her place in her chair, exhausted but satisfied. She looked at me and said, "That's my father."

"An anxious man," I answered.

"You've got it. Really—and out to lunch."

"And your mother?" I asked quickly, seizing the opportunity while she was talkative.

Marda slumped back into her chair, burying her head in her coat. I thought I had lost her again when she suddenly leaped to her feet, charged toward me, grabbed my shoulders, and shook me, shouting, "Give me, give me, give me!"

My impulse was to defend myself by pushing her away, but before I could do so, she had stopped, apologetic. "Oh, what am I doing? I didn't mean to be so aggressive. I'm truly sorry. But I felt so much relief in showing you my father, I guess I got carried away in giving you a picture of my mother. I'm truly sorry." She helped straighten my blouse and reached for my hands, holding them, wishing desperately to make amends.

"It's all right," I told her, holding her hands. Suddenly aware of our contact, she immediately withdrew her hands, returned to her chair, and sat stone faced. "I'd better go," she told me, pulling her coat more tightly around her. She looked at my clock on the wall. "The session is over anyway. I'd like to come back next week. Will you work with me again? But I can't stay now. It's too much."

"I would like to work with you, Marda," I said earnestly, looking into her blue eyes. This time she did not lower them. She put her head down, smiling shyly.

"I would like to work with your body the next time you come," I added. "That will prepare you for serious therapeutic work."

She nodded, keeping her head lowered as she left my office.

I had the feeling that our brief interaction had become a sweet secret within her, which she would cherish for the coming week.

3

Explaining the Modality

I had explained to Marda that her work with me would involve an analytic process that required not only speaking about one's problems but working with the "armoring" of the body as well. Marda had heard about the methodology of Bioenergetics from the woman who referred her to me. Marda had sought me out.

In her next session I asked her to undress but to remain in her underwear and brassiere. Marda took a long time. I sensed she was uncomfortable being exposed.

I urged her to step before the large mirror. She did so, but turned quickly away from her own image. I asked her to look at her face and body and tell me what she felt about it.

Marda stole a hasty glance at her image in the mirror. Immediately she began to rub her hands together in an obsessive manner, much like the portrayal of her father in her previous session. She continued this action, alternately placing the palms of her hands over her eyes and then rubbing them together again. She was sweating profusely. I had never witnessed such agony in my many years of therapeutic work.

"Marda," I said softly, "we can do this another time."

"No, it won't be different another time. You can see that I hate myself, all of me—always have and always will. It's been like this since I was born. I hate all of me—my body, my mind, everything about me. I don't want to be on this Earth or in this body."

"You are a beautiful young woman, Marda," I said gently.

"That's what they all tell me. Who cares for a beautiful body and face? I don't. Who cares, when I feel so rotten inside?"

I wondered how I could reach this anguished soul. After a moment I asked her to draw on a sheet of paper her perception of her internal rottennesss.

"I can't draw," she told me.

"You can feel the rottenness. Draw what you feel and it will express your state."

She took the paper and pencil and viciously drew lines extending from the top of the paper to the bottom and from one side to the other. With the point of the pencil she put a hole into the center of the paper, then stuck the pencil through it.

"There. Is that what you want?" she asked defiantly.

"Pretty furious feelings, Marda. Where in your body do you feel them?" I asked as I looked at the drawing, wondering where to begin my therapeutic work.

"Here," she said as she pointed to her genitals. "Here." She pointed in turn to her diaphragm, chest, shoulder girdle, neck, jaw, eyes, forehead.

"What does your body feel like?" I asked.

"Like this!" she told me, facing the mirror and contracting the areas she had indicated. "These places are thick and stiff, like a wall that's impenetrable."

"Why did you create such a wall?" I asked.

"Because I don't want *her* near me. I don't want *him* near me, either. About him I'm not sure. But I'm sure about her."

"Would you like to release some of those rotten feelings? I can put you over the breathing stool to elicit breathing. That will bring feelings to the surface. Do you want to penetrate that wall so you'll feel better about yourself?"

"Sometimes I want it; most of the time I don't. I'm not only rotten, I'm a coward." She paused. After a few minutes of silent suffering she said: "I'll try."

Marda went to the stool. She arched over it, touching the areas of her body that were filled with her furious feelings. I positioned her so, one by one, those areas she felt were stuck were directly over the stool. Her body was so rigid and unbreathing that she looked like a wooden board on top of it. She panicked, flew off the stool, stood immobilized in front of me: ashen, eyes closed, arms held tightly by her sides, legs and thighs clenched together. She was breathless.

I went to her quickly and held her. Slowly her body unstiffened; she breathed more fully. She jumped away from me. Her eyes were slits. She began to mumble in a sing-song fashion:

> I'm inside, inside, inside,
> Seldom outside.
> No one can get to me.
>
> You think you see me,
> You really don't.
> 'Cause I won't let you in.
>
> I'm tucked away,
> It's safe and dull
> On the inside, inside, inside.

Her voice was that of a child. She sang this song three times. It reminded me somehow of her hand-rubbing gesture.

After the third time, relief came to her. She felt safer. Her song, I realized, was clearly her way of recreating her physical and emotional armor.

"You're sneaky, Anneliese," she said eventually. "You thought you would get me to breathe and release, didn't you?"

"Yes, that was my intention. You want to change, don't you? That's why you are here. You don't want to be stuck forever on the inside, inside, inside, never going outside in a true way, never taking risks with living, do you?"

"That's why I'm here. Be patient with me. Perhaps the next time I'll be less of a 'golem.'"

"A what?"

"A 'golem'—it means buried inside. That's the image that came to me while I was over the breathing stool. I never knew that about my state. Pretty graphic! Pretty awful!"

"They must have had an overwhelming impact on you?"

"My parents?"

"Yes. What happened?"

"They weren't too different from anyone else's, I guess. But they did leave their mark."

"For the next session, I should like you to be ready to look at your parents, bringing your feelings about them into the open. Doing so will clarify the confusion in you—confusion and tension you've been subject to from birth. You got yoked to their negative behavior—as all people do with their parents. You do not want to go on like this forever, do you?"

"No," said Marda, hanging her head. "I'll bring out whatever memories come to the surface." She smiled a childlike smile and, again with lowered head, left my office.

"Bye," she said before shutting the door, giving me a last warm glance.

"Goodbye, Marda," I waved. "See you next week."

4

Marda's Environment

Marda came into the next session with drawings that represented the environment she grew up in. She proudly gave them to me, as if to tell me she wasn't always hidden inside, that she wanted to come out of her shell and live a more productive life.

I felt her effort, but when she took her seat opposite mine there was a sudden shift in her feelings, evidenced by the difference in her energy. I looked up from the drawings to find that she was no longer "visible." She had gone inside her "golem" habitat. She tried to smile, but her lowered head indicated that her efforts at consciousness were eroding quickly.

"Marda," I called to her. "Marda, let me help you stay visible." She shook her head. Her chest heaved slightly, her mouth twitched, her eyes fluttered, her hands began to rub against each other.

"Lie on the bed," I urged softly. "Let yourself be wherever you are. It's safe in my office. Let your feelings come to the surface. You won't have to hide them anymore."

I took her icy hands in mine and brought her to the bed near my desk. I palpated her chest and abdomen, helping to stimulate the breathing in her body. She turned her face toward the wall. The heaving of her chest gave way to gentle crying, which she tried in vain to hold back. The more I stimulated her breathing, the less was she able to remain inside herself.

"Let your feelings out, Marda," I pleaded. "Let them out. They will remain poisonous if you keep them locked inside. You promised you were going to share your background with me. Do you remember?"

Her face turned toward me, her tear-stained eyes closed. She was whimpering.

"How old are you, Marda?" I asked.

"Five. Maybe eight."

"What's happening?" I prodded, encouraged by her response.

"Cold, cold—in my bed. My brother Ivan's on the other side of the room. A little older. Don't know him, don't want to. My mother likes him. Noise in the house. Many Communist people—all talking at once. About bombs—the 'cold war.' What's war? I don't know; it's bad. Feel very cold and scared. Scared the police will come, take us away; scared the house will be blown up. I cry some, but no one comes. My brother's scared, too, but he doesn't do anything."

Marda was silent. Her brows were contracted. I could feel something brewing. Soon the following sounds and words: "*Mmmmmmm, rrrrrrrr*—rip you, rip you apart, slap you down, poke you, slap you, *mmmmmmmm*, stupid, stupid—man—huh—man—what man, where are you? Where are you? Nothing! Nothing! Ever, ever. See me? See me? No! You never see me!"

Suddenly Marda made fists that she poked into the air. She became red in the face as she gesticulated: "Who cares if your mother wouldn't feed you? Who cares if she didn't give you money for medicine when you were sick? Who cares that she threw you out of your home into the cold wintry night because you couldn't work? Who cares? You're an alcoholic zombie. Why did you marry my mother? 'The thing to do?' What about me? *Me*? Your daughter, whom you didn't see, never, never. Never touched. Rip you open. Apart. Rip you!"

Marda was breathing heavily, thrashing on the bed as though she were ripping her father apart. She regained her normal consciousness and was on the verge of retreating inside herself when I told her to open her mouth and breathe like a fish out of water. Following my instructions, she stayed with me.

"Go on, Marda," I urged. "Go on with whatever feelings come to the surface. You've been hiding them your entire life. Let them come up so you can have more awareness of who you really are."

Marda was breathing deeply through her mouth. The flow of energy through her encountered many of the physical blocks in her body. The most severe at this moment was the throat block.

"Can't talk," she said. Her voice was raspy. "My tongue, my tongue. It's going to the back of my throat—like someone's pulling it back. Help me. I'm going to choke."

"Stick it out as far out as you can," I instructed. "Open your mouth wide and let me help release it from the back of your throat." I held on to the tip of her tongue and pulled gently, so she would feel its presence in her mouth instead of imagining being strangled by it. Relieved, she held my hands in hers, grateful.

Soon she closed her eyes again, open to more feelings. "Mother? Mother? You're there but I can't tell you anything. I can't tell you I'm hurting because you're hurting more than me. You felt closer to Ivan because he looked like you—had your beaked nose. Mine's like my father's. We're handsome and you were always jealous.

"Can't talk to you, so I hold back. Hold back my tongue; it gets caught in the back of my throat, as if I'd rather choke than say what I feel. You were always hurting. Why did you marry him—that drunk? You joked about his consenting to have sex with you twice in your life—once to have Ivan and the second time to have me. Why didn't you leave?

"I'm confused about you. I know I don't want to be touched by you. Keep your hands off me. I feel as though you want to grab me, to eat me alive. You're a cannibal, eating your own flesh because you don't have enough of yourself. No wonder—you had a crazy mother and a father who died when you were little and now you're with a zombie who gives nothing. Well, I'm not your nurturance—I'm barely alive myself. So lay off. Feed off Ivan. He wants it. I don't."

Marda was deathly silent, digesting uneasily what she had said about her mother. Becoming conscious of her feelings put Marda into a raw state, a state she denied herself most of the time. It jolted her, but she could not deny her distaste for her mother.

"Well, Marda," I said, breaking into the long silence that followed her rejection of her mother, "that's a good glimpse of your background."

"I guess. I'm trying to stay with my feelings, but it's hard."

"You can stay with what happened today by writing it down. If you decide to go into your shell, you can always refer to your notes. Soon you will want to stay more conscious. For the present, absorb whatever you can, believing that you can come out of your maze to find yourself a powerful person."

"Thanks. Don't forget to look at my drawings. Bye."

5

Marda's Impressions

6

Marda Was a Challenge

Marda was a challenge. She kept me busy finding creative therapeutic ways to prevent her from disappearing inside her psychic prison.

As her drawing on page 23 depicts, her childhood surroundings were chaotic, filled with fear, rage, hatred, coldness.

It was an atmosphere dominated by the father's alcoholism and her parents' involvement in the Communist party. This involvement kept them occupied with the party's ideology, making Marda feel she was an outsider—not only in school but also among her friends. She spent evenings in her bed, listening anxiously to the secrets of the party members congregated in the kitchen of their home. She was different from her schoolmates, though she wanted to belong, to be like everyone else. She wanted to be able to tell her friends that her parents spent the evenings with their children, listening to their stories about school, helping them with their homework, and tucking them into bed. Instead, she spent sleepless nights, isolated, terrified by the people at the meetings in their kitchen.

When her father was drunk he called his wife *stupid, whore, inhuman, bitch*. His wife fought back weakly but ultimately looked toward her children to give her comfort and acceptance. They became her allies—and victims.

Marda had found a way to stay alive: to remain locked within her fortress, looking out at the world with slitted eyes. Her brother was doted upon by their mother, infantilized by her needy caring.

According to Marda, Ivan, now an adult in his forties, lived a block away from their parents' household, visiting them several times a week. He had become friends with his father, with whom he drank heavily. Together they denigrated the mother, who sought the help of Alanon. Her only weapon was detachment, lending itself to more coldness and more distancing. The mother and father lived under the same roof like transients, wasting time, wasting energy, wasting life. Marda avoided contact with all of them.

As I worked with Marda's psyche and body, there was a gradual thawing in her nature; but many years were to pass before she was able to remain cogently in reality. The temptation to return to her fortress was ever-present. People were intrigued by her, but since she would let few get to know her, the challenge to stay out of her shell was one she seldom met.

The most dramatic event at the beginning of our work together was when Marda was fired from her first meaningful job—at a publishing company. She could not meet the demands of her female boss to write a summary of her lecture tours. Marda could not focus on her boss's achievements, no matter how hard she tried. Clearly her boss had become her demanding mother.

Once Marda was inside her wall, her feelings were foreign agents. Avoiding reality became her overriding way of coping. She was safe in her shell, except that she still had to meet her physical needs and survive in the everyday world.

The thawing continued within the framework of her ability to stay with herself and her feelings. Who is she as her shell crumbles? Who is Marda?

She comes to my office willingly now, wanting to grow, to feel her body and her self more fully. She is a beautiful woman, who turns many heads. But she still is not aware, still not in tune with that aspect of herself. She dresses sloppily, giving little attention to her appearance; her feminine image is askew.

She is heterosexual but her sexuality remains undefined; perhaps "mangled" would be a better word. It reminds me of her drawing of her genitals, with a pencil piercing the middle.

When I open the topic of a relationship with a man, she nods her head, smiles, and tells me how good it would be to be involved. She experiences a spurt of energy and asks her friends if they know an eligible man. When no possibility appears—and none ever does—she drops the matter and returns to her undefined feminine self.

Concerned over her repetitive passivity with regard to her sexual nature, I asked her to write about her sexuality—to let the unconscious take over. She smiled her usual, ingratiating smile, though I was not certain if she would come through. To my surprise, she arrived at the next session with the following poem. She read:

> It's there, but like
> my throat,
> it's choked in
> DUNG.
>
> Why DUNG?
>
> Don't know,
> except it's just
> untouchable.
>
> Choked.
> He stuck—
> What?
> When?
> Little, little baby
> stuck,
> my mouth
> my tongue pushed back

by—
no breath
my eyes popping out.

Why's he doing this?
I'm so little.

Twice bad!
Bad
Bad.

Oh, why?
why,
Daddy?

You like your little
girl,
in ways
different
from
Mom.

You touch me,
it's something,
otherwise nothing.
But,
why like this?
Like this?

I'll do it again,
to have you
touch me.
But,

I know
it's
bad,
bad,
bad.

I did not speak, being clear that I believed she was not finished. My silence grew prolonged. I waited for her to say something. It became a game of "who will speak first?"

I was determined to hold out indefinitely, so she would take responsibility for what she had read. But when I looked at her more carefully, I realized she was encased in her mummy shell. I also realized that nothing would extricate her from her shell at that time.

"Marda," I said with compassion and impatience mingled, "give thought to your poem until the next time. You came into this session having done extraordinary work. The next step is to analyze what's behind the poem, to work it through."

She stood up in a huff. "There's nothing behind it, other than what the words say. I don't feel it's anything more than that. And besides, it could be my imagination—nothing more."

She put on her coat and left, slammed the door without looking back at me with her usual shy smile.

I was shocked but pleased. "At least she's not in a state of inertia," I thought. "Inertia deadens. Anger creates action."

7

The Next Session

"I was rude," Marda apologized next time we met, as she took her seat in the chair opposite mine. "But I must admit it felt good to get angry at you. I'm always trying to please you, and this time I didn't want to. Even though you were right to make me think about the poem, I just couldn't do it then."

"I accept your apology, Marda," I answered, smiling warmly. "What did you get from it?"

"Nothing much," she said, not flinching.

"Nothing much?" I echoed, attempting to hide the consternation I felt at the thought of how much energy I would have to call upon to coax her out of her willful hiding.

"It's a poem, that's all."

"You're right. It's just a poem. But let's try to understand the poem. What was your father doing?"

"How do you know it refers to my father?" Marda countered, looking at me amused.

"You referred to the man as 'daddy' didn't you?" I was bewildered, perplexed that she could have sneaked so quickly inside her fortress, where lies were a commonplace.

"It could be poetic license," she said, rubbing the palms of her hands together. "Can't we do something else? I don't feel well. Your insistent questioning makes me furious."

"Does it, Marda? Well, go to the bed and express your fury. You know how it's done by now."

She opened her mouth to protest. She looked for any softening in my demeanor, but I sat like a rock.

She went to the bed, took a tennis racquet into her hands, held it behind her head. She was about to vent her fury when she eyed me appealingly, making one more attempt to engage my sympathy.

I shouted: "Hit, Marda! Hit! Let your fury out at me, if that's where it belongs. But, hit! Don't hold back."

Marda dropped the racquet, sat on the edge of the bed. She became a child before my eyes. She rubbed her unfocused eyes, peering at me through slits. She almost gurgled.

I went to her. *My God, what did they do to this person?* I held her in my arms. "It's all right, Marda. It's all right. You'll not be punished for saying what you feel."

Her hands crept tentatively along my chest. I could feel the fear that enveloped her action. I placed my hands on top of hers, letting her know that I welcomed her touch.

When she was sure I would not hurt her, her hands continued their exploration until they embraced my upper back. She pressed me close to her body. I returned the pressure of her touch and rocked her.

She smiled and cooed, "Nice baby. Nice baby. A good, good baby. Nice, nice, and pretty, too."

We remained like this for some time. Marda was totally involved in cooing and gurgling and other baby talk. As she imbibed my warmth and acceptance, I became the nurturer she had never had. That gap in her makeup was healing and her confidence was being restored. She was finally satisfied.

I waited for her to make the next move. She became agitated. Then she suddenly sprung out of my lap, pushed me away from the bed, took the racquet, and hit the bed, screaming: "Where were you, Mother? Why didn't you rock me and cuddle me as this woman is doing? Where were you? You're always pulling at *me* to get affection!

"I'm little and you're big; *you* should be comforting *me*. And another thing, I'm not your rival. I'm your child! You don't want me to be beautiful. You don't want *him* to think I'm beautiful. You don't want me to be successful. You just want me there, to be used by you. You're disgusting. No wonder I don't want to look at the poem. Distorted as his behavior was, it felt like affection—more than I got from you."

She threw the racquet on the bed, returned to her chair, opposite mine. "It took a while, but I got there," she exclaimed, out of breath, exuberant.

"Okay, Marda," I responded. "Now let's talk about your history with men."

"Almost nonexistent," she replied readily, "even though I'm supposed to be 'beautiful.' I'm orgasmic—there's nothing wrong with me physiologically; it's all psychological." She paused for a long time. "I feel confused and I have to ask you some questions. How do I know the feelings in that poem are real? How do I know such a thing happened? How could my father do such a thing?"

"The feelings are real because they came from your unconscious," I explained. "When you wrote the poem, something clicked within you, a truth that cannot be denied, a truth that had to emerge in order for you to move beyond where you are."

"But why would he do such a thing?" She was pleading, not wishing to relinquish her illusions about him.

"Within the human psyche is a great deal of evil. What prompted the evil to become active in him? Frustration, drunken stupor, hatred toward the feminine? Who knows? One thing is certain—it was depravity."

Marda listened, struggling not to retreat from this unwelcome reality. I appreciated her effort.

"Ground yourself, Marda. Stand, feel the ground underneath your feet. Feel the energy of the earth going through your body as an anchor to your being. You want to face your realities from a grounded position. Groundedness will not allow you to split off from yourself; it will help prevent you from going into your habitual refuge."

She listened. I sensed she was with me. I proceeded: "How do you expect to get beyond this block with men?"

"Don't know," she answered. "Magically, a man will pop up. Always has."

"How long have you been thinking like this?"

"Ever since . . . ."

"When?"

"Ever since I was involved with a married man—an executive—my second job. He was passionate. I was flattered. He was my boss and much older. He'd go home after our sex was finished. I didn't object. Didn't know there could be more. Never asked. Eventually, he rejected me. Said I was beautiful and sexy, but 'not there.'"

"How did you feel?"

"Awful. Took years to get over the hurt. Then I waited for another man to appear. He did. He was shorter than me, which bothered me, but devoted—almost smothering. He lived on the West Coast, so we didn't have consistent contact. I would see him when he came to the city. It was nice, but afterwards I was always tired and depressed. Because of the distance between us, the relationship just evaporated. I guess I didn't yearn for it too much. I don't seem to have too much active desire for any man. It's buried inside."

I felt Marda's involvement with her story. In order not to lose her, I reminded her that she had met Georgio, her next lover. He had attended my classes and was also seeing me professionally, as a client.

"Yeah," said Marda. "That relationship was hopeful at first, because he was also doing Bioenergetic therapy with you. We even had those sessions with you together. Then one day he said he wanted to end his relationship with me. I wanted to die. He had held out to conquer me; the moment I surrendered, he was gone. He left me, the therapy, the city. I was raw. Up to then the therapy had made me more accessible, but after Georgio left, I really shut down."

"You were clear that he was not ready for a serious relationship. Why has it taken another eight years for you to even think about another man? You say you want children and marriage. What happened in the interim?"

"I go into my shell. You know my history with jobs until the present one, which is demanding. Everything else becomes more important than a relationship. I want a relationship, but it becomes a distant desire. The longer I stay away from men, the more distant the desire becomes."

"What is in the way, Marda?" I asked. "What is the block?"

She became silent. She grounded ferociously, breathed deeply, making every effort to stay connected. After a long pause, she said, "I guess it's my father. I want him—always did. He wasn't available, but I wanted him. Don't understand it, but I can't hate him. I should. I don't want to hate him. He's my father."

I took a long, deep breath, not wishing to interfere with her availability, and hoped my instincts would serve me. I brought logic to her emotional state: "Did he support you, Marda? Send you to college? Did he hold you, cherish you, teach you?"

"'No' to all of it!" she admitted quietly. "But I just can't let go of him."

"Why not?"

"Don't know. I become blank and all men fit into the blank. When there's a blank, there's no reason to do anything and the 'not doing anything' becomes eternal."

"Do you think," I volunteered delicately, "that the early sexual abuse created a bond between you and your father?"

"Could be," she answered. A spark of revelation made her body jerk. "You mean a bond with the male? You mean I hold on to that bond because I couldn't bond with my mother?"

"Terrific, Marda," I said quietly. "Go on."

Her resistance had vanished. "Yes, that must be it. I couldn't bond with my mother for fear she'd eat me alive. So I held on to the horror he engaged me in, even though I was little."

"You're saying it, Marda. That bond, established in infancy, keeps you wed to him—forever. And your life will be wasted if you continue to nurture the illusion that this connection was one of love."

"Not entirely," Marda argued. "At least I've got something to hold on to. A male image! Unwholesome as it is, it's male and it's important, because I don't want any part of *her* energy."

"True. But you've sacrificed yourself to have his male energy. You have sacrificed your own female energy because you want none of hers. The naked truth, however, is that you reflect them both. When you understand this truth, you will wonder if the sacrifice is worth it. We'll deal with the concept of Reflectivism in the next session. In the meantime, you have stayed present with a difficult issue, and you have not perished, have you? On the contrary, you seem to be more alive than I have ever seen you. Do you agree?"

"I've got to say yes. But the burning question is, why have I been so susceptible to accepting so much distortion—their distortion—in this life? Why have I allowed myself to become a zombie, like both of them? Why have I continued with the lie that they were there for me, when they were so absent—so unbelievably absent?"

"Excellent questions, Marda. Think about them."

"I will. You're right. I haven't died and I don't want to. But I'm tired, bone tired. It's strange, though I look forward to the next time I see you."

"I do, too, Marda. Goodbye."

8

What a Dream!

It was Sunday, two o'clock in the morning. The phone rang. I answered, half-awake.

Marda's voice was on the line. She apologized profusely for disturbing me, saying she had never thought she would do what she was doing. Please forgive her.

"Marda," I responded, "tell me if you're all right."

"Yes," she said. "Now I feel silly for doing this, but it seemed so important to talk to you."

"Marda, you have called me. I'm awake and I am ready to listen to what you have to say, so please say it. I don't want to have to coax it from you. Besides, I'm very interested in hearing what's come up. Now please tell me. I'm sure it's important."

"Well, I had a dream—or I think it was a dream. It felt so real that I still don't know if I was awake or asleep. It was as if angels painted images in my mind, like telepathy. They spoke in a strange rhythm and poetic language to convey what they needed to say. It took me a while to get accustomed to the fact that what I was hearing and seeing was real. Once I got used to it, though, it felt like a normal way to perceive things."

"That's interesting. Did you write down what you learned?"

"Yes. Do you want to hear? I think it relates to the question I asked before I left your office."

"You wondered why you persisted in your illusion that your parents were there for you," I responded, eager to hear about her dream.

"Oh, you do remember, don't you? That makes me feel very good. Well, here it is."

She sounded transported to another realm as the following emerged:

> *Little boy, Ronald, from the*
> *city of London,*
> *the time in the*
> *last century.*
> *So sweet, so young,*
> *blond and handsome.*
> *That is what your mummy thought*
> *of you.*
>
> *She loves you,*
> *an illegitimate babe,*
> *product of her*
> *whoring life—*
> *the sperm from a ship's*
> *captain.*
>
> *The night conception happened*
> *she heard the angels sing,*
> *though angels are not*
> *welcome in a whorehouse.*
> *The mother knew,*
> *expectant and hopeful.*
> *Her dreams were filled*
> *with the captain's image.*
>
> *She sings to you*
> *while you're still in her womb:*

*"My little babe,
a captain you'll become,
like your father who
sails the seas.
He'll bring you toys
from distant lands,
and tell you stories,
miraculous to hear.*

*"He'll take you with him
when you are older.
A valiant sailor
you'll become.
He'll look at you,
taking pride in his
offspring—
He'll see his image—
like father, like son."*

*The captain becomes aware
your mummy has born him a son.
He is kind to her.
Mummy looks on
with love,
but
he does not care—
so selfish is
his nature.*

*You resemble him—
it cannot be denied.
His love grows for you.*

*He runs to the brothel,
takes you in his arms,
but alas, his homecomings
are seldom.*

*She tries to raise you
in a decent manner,
but her life is chaotic.
You roam
the streets of London,
terrified and alone.
No one
but the whores
accepts you.*

*The day comes
when your mummy
becomes sick.
You see her lying in
her bed.
She coughs so hard that
her body convulses.
She stares at you
with glazed eyes.
The breath leaves her body.
She dies.*

*You look on—
bewildered.
You are only ten.
The whores are too busy
to take care of you.*

MARDA

*You remain beside
her cold body.
Tearless.
Alone.*

*Dazedly,
you walk the streets,
until months later
the captain fortuitously
reappears in London.
He hears the story.
He looks you over.
"Come lad," he says,
"you'll be with me
and live the life of
a sailor."*

*You try to smile,
but your face and your soul
are frozen.
"Cheer up," he says,
patting you on the back.
"You've got a father—
you'll not be an
orphan."*

*You go with him,
following like a
puppy.
"Hurry!" he shouts,
looking back.
"There's the ship.*

*Isn't she a beauty?
You'll sleep in the
captain's room with me."*

*You follow,
but your heart is
with your mummy.
The bond between you
and the captain is fragile.
At first he is patient—
he understands your pain,
and often humors you
out of it.*

*You are not a good sailor.
He loses patience.
He disappears into his cabin
and drinks.
He leaves you alone
most of the time.
All of it—
reminiscent of the
streets of London.*

*You are fearful, sick,
and forlorn.
The other sailors are
gruff and insensitive.
They call you the captain's
bastard.*

*You look to the captain
for a little love,
but he is disgusted*

by your frailty.
You stay by yourself
most of the time.
Sometimes he is
remorseful.
But when you show fear
or a need for him,
he turns his back
and rejects you again.

One day you climb
the mast.
It is high and slick.
You grasp it tightly
with all your ten-year-old's
strength.
The mast sways in
a gale that
springs up from nowhere.
You are frightened, but
aware of a new resolve—
that life without love
is unbearable.

You look at the water
beneath,
mesmerized.
You long for it
as you long for
your mummy's womb.
You will be safe there—
not lonely.

*You hear
the captain shout:
"Get down here!"*

*You look down at him
with his roaring, cold
voice.
You look at the
water below.
Your fingers let go—
the mast sways
violently.
Your body finds
its place in the sea.*

*Down, down you go—
a smile on your lips.
No longer will you
feel lonely.
You will be safe
in the water's bosom—*

*Existence will be
painless—
at last!*

    Marda stopped speaking. There was a deep, long silence. I heard her breathing heavily on the other end of the line; she was trying not to sob.

    "Let it out, Marda," I encouraged tenderly.

    "Oh, God! God! God!" she wailed. "Have pity on my little Ronald—the part of me that is so lonely, so unwilling to be in life. You're at the core of my being, always deeply alone and lonely. Ronald, you're waiting to be recognized by me. I want to hold you, rock you, coddle you as you never were by them. I want to bring you back to life. Come out, out of that cold, dark sea and become a part of me. Little forlorn Ronald, let me love you. I'll take care of you from now on. You're a vital part of me—the child I forsook, they forsook. Oh, God! Help me give him life."

"Take a blanket, Marda," I interrupted. "Fold it, take it into your arms, continue with your imagery. Bring Ronald, in the form of the blanket, close to you and give him all the love your heart is capable of giving. Bring him to life."

"I have a blanket," she said, totally involved with the child inside her. "I'm rocking him. It feels so real and I love him so much. It's a love I never felt before. It's a love that comes from a bright red heart, a heart filled with goodness."

Marda was healing her disconnection to the forlorn, lost Ronald inside her.

"I feel so much better," she said after a few moments. "It's like a piece of me got resurrected."

"Our psyches are like jigsaw puzzles; we find piece after piece until the puzzle is complete."

"I agree."

"I hope you realize, Marda, what a miracle your 'dream' was—if you want to call it that. You seem to have been blessed by your unconscious, by the angels, or by whatever name you choose to call your divine assistance. Have you ever had such an experience before?"

"You're wondering if God ever spoke to me before?" she asked, a defiant, cynical tone suddenly in her voice.

"Yes," I answered.

"God!" she repeated scornfully. "I had a dream. That's all. It came at the right time. I've got to go now. It's three in the morning. Thanks for your time." She hung up the phone.

I felt Marda had put me in a box, a box with a beautiful ribbon around it, a box with a label that said "NOT TO BE OPENED UNTIL I SAY SO."

I called upon my own angels and asked them why I had been destined to help this particular soul. The answer that came was:

> *It is a soul you spurned*
> *not once or twice,*
> *but many times.*
>
> *It follows then that*
> *you must rectify,*
> *and help her*
> *to become*
> *mortal.*

9

Reflectivism: The Female Energy

Marda came into my office on her next visit looking at me sheepishly. Like a timid, wary animal, she sniffed out the lay of the land. I could feel her antennae probing the air to pick up signals from me. Chastened by the rebuke she'd given me at the end of her previous session, I decided to roll up my sleeves and go to work.

"I did it again," Marda apologized as she took her seat. "I was rude, so inconsiderate. You gave me your time at two in the morning, and I acted like a brat. What's the matter with me? Why do I go in and out of my shell? Why does the word 'God' send me into such a rage? Is it my atheistic background? Why, Anneliese? I'm so sorry. Please forgive me."

"I forgive you, Marda," I said, impressed by her awareness and sincerity. "We have work to do, so let's get busy. Let's make you mortal."

"What?" she asked.

"Mortal, Marda. *Real, in life . . . alive . . . conscious . . . human . . . excited about living . . . and divine.*"

"I want all of that, but I'm a long way from the divine," she said, smiling.

"You never know," I replied mischievously. I knew she would have preferred to chew and rechew her inability to be present, blaming her parents for her isolated life. It was time to push her beyond blame and victimization.

"You've been in therapy for eight years, Marda, in which time you have become aware of the disastrous effect your environment had on your psyche."

"They were horrible people," she whined.

"As you say that, notice what is happening to your psyche and your body."

"I feel very little, and weepy, and I want to go to you and be held. I want you to rock me and I want to talk baby talk. That would be heaven."

"How long would you like to be in this state?" I asked.

"Forever. I'm justified, aren't I? After all, look at what they did to me!"

"Their abuse was inexcusable, but you will remain a justified victim of their abuse—using it as your badge of honor, your modus operandi, your reason for not moving further—if you insist on staying where you are." I made a decisive move. "Which of your parents is the weepy, cold victim?"

"My mother!" she said quickly.

"What other adjectives can you apply to your mother?"

"*Weepy! . . . Cold! . . . Willful! . . . Martyr! . . . Tyrannical within her martyrdom!* Oh, how I hate her. How I don't want to be anything like her."

I smiled. "We all spend a lifetime avoiding being like the hateful parent or parents. But the energy we use being different from them puts such a magnified focus on them that we never get away from them. We never *do* get away from them until our consciousness can accept that we reflect them. We choose them prenatally to recognize that their unsavory qualities are in us. This is what I have come to believe, and it's a powerful idea. This truth will enable us to rectify and then to claim our true identity, and our Godself."

"Are you saying I'm like her? And what do you mean, 'Godself'?" she asked, wild with disbelief.

"Yes, Marda. You reflect her. And your father as well. And yes, you are a part of God. We all have the innate but unconscious desire to return to that divinity. The sooner we recognize these facts, the less karma we will accumulate and the faster we will become whole."

Marda sat speechless; she sputtered but could not get the words out. She did not go into her shell; she was taken off-guard. I seized the opportunity to explain the concept of Reflectivism.

"Be grateful for the realization that you are like your mother. Now you can rectify and reclaim your true female energy. Once it's reclaimed, you will find the real, feminine Marda, the true divine female spark that God created."

"Stop saying 'God'," she screamed. "I want nothing to do with Him. When you say that word I want to hide, hide so I'm never visible, so I don't see Him and He doesn't see me." She suddenly fell silent. "Maybe He's the reason I concocted my 'golem' shell. Oh, it's such a puzzle!"

"The puzzle will become clearer. Let's go hunting in your unconscious for another female, one who will explain you to yourself more clearly, a part that will enable you to change your concept of your female, redeem her, and bring her to another kind of consciousness."

"Okay," said Marda, exhausted but willing to change her present state. "What must I do?"

"Go to the bed, lie down, connect to your body by breathing deeply. Watch the flow of your breath and bring it to the armored parts of your body, so those parts too can become engaged. When you and your body are connected, listen to my voice and follow its instructions."

Marda obeyed. When her body was prone and relaxed, her eyes closed. I began to speak soothingly.

"You are safe, Marda. I am by your side. You will have an adventure that will bring your consciousness to another place, a place from which you can learn about your true self, a place that will give you an extraordinary experience. Yearn for such an experience, because it will enlighten you." I saw the movement beneath her closed eyelids and knew it indicated that she was ready to speak.

"A strong, compelling force is pulling me away from here," she began. "It feels like my experience with little Ronald. I see a cave."

"Go into the cave, Marda, and look around."

"I wander into it," she responded, filled with curiosity.

"What do you see?"

"Lots and lots of books, all colors, all shapes and sizes," she said excitedly.

"Choose one of the books, one that really intrigues you."

"I'm choosing one with my name written on the outside. It's written in gold letters. My name is so impressive in gold. I could look at it forever."

"Open it," I said, though sensing she wanted to go no farther.

"I'm scared to pick it up and open it."

"Don't stop now, Marda. Be courageous. Pick it up and turn to the first page."

"I'm doing so, but I feel as though I'm in a dream. My body seems to want to fall into the pages of the book. Here I go. I'm not going to fight this. I do fall into the pages of the book. It's as though the book and I become one. I lose my connection to now and to the me that is in the now." Her voice faded away. She lightly touched her body all over. "I'm becoming someone else." She fell silent, trying to assess where she was, but she was now submerged in another existence.

"Where are you? Who are you?" I asked softly. "What is happening?"

I'm tall like me, and beautiful,
dignified,
proud and haughty,
from a rich family
in a medieval city.

Something is wrong.
Something is amiss.
I walk but I stumble
whenever I'm on my
feet.
What ails me?
I'm only twenty-two.

*Someone's hand is
always available.
Why should this be?
I'm a grown woman.
Tell me, someone,
"What is wrong with me?"*

*"You're blind,"
they tell me.
"Blind?" I ask.
"Blind, our child.
You cannot see."*

*They tell me this
wherever I go.
"That's preposterous,"
I insist.
"You're blind,
beautiful woman.
You cannot see."*

*I strike that blunt stranger
until he falls.
I kick at his body,
though I see him not.
"How dare you mock
me?"
I scream at him.
"You'll pay for your
lies."*

*My parents have him
punished.
He spends a year in prison.*

*I relish my vengeance
in my hardened heart.
"No one dares
contradict me."*

*"You should be wed,"
my parents tell me.
"You're too easily
overwrought."
They find me a
suitable mate.
He appears one day
as I sit in the garden.
He approaches and
is smitten.*

*He is a good man,
his sensibilities refined.
He marvels at my beauty
along with my denial
of my state.
He perceives it as courage,
not fear.
He wishes to bring me joy
and to take care
of me.*

*I am happy at first,
for I can feel his love,
but my blocked heart
cannot accept what he
gives.*

*He is patient
with my abuse.
He blames
my affliction.
"What affliction?"
I shout,
when he attempts
to bring me to reason.*

*"There is no affliction,"
I scream until
I'm exhausted.
"No affliction!
Do you hear?
Never tell me
I am impaired.
I'll have you mutilated
until you die."*

*He does not leave.
He continues
to love me.
Why?
I cannot fathom why.
I'm cruel to him,
disdainful, hurtful.
He smiles.
Could he be a god?*

*He becomes ill.
I am enraged.
His attention is no longer
mine alone.
I rave and rant.*

*How dare he be sick
when I am in need!*

*No doctor can cure him.
He leaves this Earth.
My heart becomes more
bitter.
"You wouldn't have
died,
if you had truly loved me.
I'll never forgive you.
Be damned forever."*

*My bitterness grows
until it consumes me.
I too die,
cursing my husband
and God.*

*"Nothing You can do
for me will avenge
my rage,"
I say to God.
"I detest living.
I deny life.
I am separate
from You."*

*I leave my body
but refuse
to enter God's heaven.
I remain blind,*

> *unwilling to open my eyes.*
>
> *I blame my affliction on God.*

A tear rolled down Marda's cheek. I allowed her to stay in this very difficult place for a long time.

Finally she came back to herself. She sat up, wiped her cheek, and said: "Mother, you pale by comparison to what I have just learned about myself. It's not easy to take this in, but I have to. I am weary, Anneliese, so weary. I'm weary because I've probably lived like this for centuries. What a waste, what a killer of life—like you, Mother, but I surpass even you. Thanks, Anneliese, for insisting I stop the pattern of destruction."

"Your efforts are valiant, Marda. If you need me, please call. I'd also like you to join my group, which meets every other Monday. I believe you already know some of the members, and I feel that your attending at this time would give you further insights into yourself, as well as a connection to other people on the road to self-discovery. It's a dynamic support system and will help someone who's been as isolated as you have. You're really ready for it."

"I was hoping you would ask me. I'd be happy to join. I'll be scared, but I'll try," said Marda, both exuberant and exhausted. "Now I want to go home and be with myself."

"Remember, Marda, I am here if you need me."

"I know. Thank you."

10

Marda and the Group

It was group time. Marda was punctual and sat in the farthest corner of the room. She knew many of the people in the group, yet tonight she chose to isolate herself from them. They streamed in one by one and, when they saw her, they hailed her, hugged her, and told her how welcome she was. She remained unmoved, her hands clasped, her fingers pulling at each other. I surmised that she resorted to this gesture instead of the habitual and more obvious palm-rubbing in order to appear normal.

I greeted her warmly, asking her how the week went. She looked at me as though she was a drowning person.

"You must feel like you are back in your family, Marda," I said, hoping to bring her to reality.

She shook her head in disbelief that I could read her feelings. "How did you know?" she asked, coming to life.

"It doesn't take much discernment," I told her. "Almost everyone would feel like you do, stepping into a large group of people."

She joined the group. A realization had apparently clicked in her that made her want to be present.

I introduced her officially to the group members, telling them that she had recently discovered she was a reflection of her mother. Sensitive to the difficulties of such a discovery, each of the members greeted her in the form of his or her own reflected female energy. They dramatized this energy with their bodies, aware of both the muscular and emotional distortions the feminine energy was trapped in. Since they had worked with the concept of Reflectivism for a long time, their portrayal of their own mothers' unwanted energy in them was no longer a threat, but a welcome realization. They experienced again and again that they could truly separate themselves from the parental influence and reclaim their intrinsic female self. They knew that rectification was not only possible but also necessary, and that such rectification led to the uncovering of their true Self.

"Show us yours," one of the members urged Marda when everyone else's reflective self had been seen.

"I couldn't," she sputtered piteously. "She's too ghastly."

"We're not here to judge one another, but to learn from one another," a male member urged. "We showed you ours!"

"Trust us!" said someone else.

"Okay! I'll try!" She stood up. The conflict in her was visible, almost overwhelming. I wondered if she would she resort to the gurgling baby, the "golem" . . . or if she would bravely expose her unsavory female nature. I wanted to help her all I could.

I told her to stretch her left arm into the air and let it fall where instinct took it. Surprised by my instructions, she did so. Without forethought, she dropped her left arm to her side, then bared her teeth, pressed her thighs and legs tightly together, and began to whimper through her clenched jaw. She twisted her body from side to side, her eyes closed. A rasping sound tore from her throat, like the sound of a saw going through green wood.

"Speak!" the group members encouraged in unison. "Speak!"

Through her clenched teeth, Marda rasped, "I'll kill you all—men, women, everyone. I'll kill you for making life so hard. Poor me! Poor me! God, it's Your fault. I hate You! I don't want to be seen in this way. I'll hide from you rather than be exposed. Only my needy self will be visible; my neediness will engage your sympathy. That makes me safe. I can hide forever while I whimper my way through life."

Marda was pensive, reflecting on what had just happened.

"Terrific, Marda," I responded supportively. "You really got to the bottom of your 'golem' self. How do you feel?"

"Weird, but better. I've nothing more to hide. I exposed it—the secret's out. I don't have to hide anymore."

"Now let us look for the intrinsic self," I said, turning to the group. "Look for the *real* female self—the part of you that you will live from."

Marda watched as the members returned to their seats, assuming an upright sitting position with closed eyes. She did the same, not knowing what to expect. I asked them to invite a higher energy—a revelatory energy wiser than themselves.

In a matter of minutes, they shared their experiences.

"I am wise, soft, giving," said one person.

"I am angry, but my anger has compassion," said another.

"I want the truth of who I am, nothing less."

"I want to learn to love you despite your transgressions."

"I reject you in me, Mother, and me in you," said Marda, pulled into the magical atmosphere in the room. "I look for the truth of myself, no matter how objectionable it might be. I prefer it, I want it, because it frees me."

The room resounded with the members' revelatory, hopeful desires to clear their psyches, to become worthy of a greater, truer Self.

I walked softly out of the room, their voices in my ears. I walked into the night, grateful to the universe for letting me help—not only myself, but also those who were searching for their Godself. I felt blessed.

11

Reflectivism: The Male Energy

I looked forward to the next session with Marda, a week later. She had broken down another barrier with the help of the group. Reaching her would be easier for me now.

"That was an amazing experience," she told me, still aglow from the feeling of not having to hide any longer. "But . . . ."

My heart sank. "But what . . . ?"

"Well—all those people talking to energies beyond this reality. It was spooky."

"You did the same, Marda. Didn't you reach someone special?"

"Yeah! Someone called 'Mary.'" Marda looked down into her lap. "You know my parents would laugh hysterically if they were to hear that an invisible energy and I were having a conversation. Both of them were anti-God, my father in particular. Probably because his horrible mother was such a devout Catholic. I'm confused."

"What was your experience with Mary?" I asked.

"It was similar to the experience I had with Ronald. She talked to me in a wise and instructive way. Almost like a good parent."

"Did your conversation with Mary continue after I left the group?"

"Yeah," said Marda slowly, holding back deliberately as if to relive the experience. "She said to let go of my father and mother, that their energies no longer served me. I kept telling her that I was afraid I would have no one at all."

"What do you feel about her advice?"

"With my mother I have no resistance; with him it's a different story—a mixed-up one."

I thought of her father's sexual molestation of Marda, of her mystifying refusal to reject it and him.

I said: "I agree with you. It is indeed a mixed-up relationship. Let's unravel the mystery by looking for another life—one in which you discover that his qualities are yours, also. How would you define him?"

Marda slitted her eyes in deep concentration as she mentally entered his psyche. Finally she uttered what she thought were the ugly adjectives describing him: *"Repressed killer, coward, a nonexistent hulk."* Then after a few moments of silence: "But now that I've defined him that way, why would I want to hold onto his image?" she asked, perplexed. "I must be crazy!"

"Not crazy, Marda. Only human. Now, I suggest you call on Mary to help you find a life that parallels his qualities."

"I know that will help me," she said.

"Lie on the bed," I told her. "Breathe deeply. Feel your body. Experience the energy, not only within you, but around you as well. Call upon Mary's help."

Marda followed my instructions. Then, after a brief pause, she asked, "Mary, can you be here for me the way you were when I discovered Ronald, and also the way you were present for me in the group? You're right. I've got to separate from my father, which means I must understand how I resemble him. Can you come to me and help me? I'd be so grateful!"

Marda reached out with her arms for Mary. From the expression on her face and her intense breathing, I felt she had made the connection. Her lips began to move slightly. She cleared her throat in order to make Mary's voice audible, as Mary spoke of another life from Marda's past . . .

MARDA

*I am a cretin,
a hulk—
huge, but
not demented.
I am a primitive
being.*

*I live with my
mother,
who has many burdens.
She martyrs herself
for me.
Deep in self-pity,
she lives out her days.*

*I'm twenty-five,
inseparable from her.
She's bossy;
I do her bidding,
like an unconscious
beast.
I grunt heavily
with every chore.*

*She looks at me
sideways,
disgusted.
"Why can't he be
normal?
He'd be wed by now.
I'd be a grandmother,
surrounded by loving
children.
Such is my fate!*

"Oh, God!
You are merciless.
I do Your Will.
But You punish me!
You took my husband.
and spared my son.
Why?

"The neighbors
mock us.
Still, he is devoted.
He helps me.
I shouldn't complain."

"Mmmmm," think I,
the hulk.
I'm without a name.
"Mmmmm," I must
obey her.
She doesn't want me.
I must be good;
I can't live
without her.

"There's much that
is wrong with me.
But my mother
should give me love.
Isn't that what
mothers do?

"I need love, Mother.
I'd not be so
forlorn."

MARDA

I follow her to and fro.
I receive her contempt.
She hides it, though,
as soon as she becomes
aware
of revealing herself.

I approach the women
in the village square.
They run from me, laughing.
I'm awkward, ugly,
needy—
I don't blame them.
But I'm so
lonely.

I go back home.
My mother's at the
hearth,
cooking our evening
meal.
She groans and moans
within herself.
I hear it somehow,
though it's inaudible.

My nerves are taut.
I feel so deprived—
deprived of someone's
loving touch.
My mind becomes splintered.
I take an axe.
I hit her on her

head.
She falls to the ground—
dead.

I gaze on her lifeless body.
I feel no remorse
I bury her in the fields.
"You were my mother,
but you're gone.
I'm glad.
I have no regrets."

No one asks about her.
When they do—
I tell them she's
visiting her sister.
I live by myself,
but,
I continue to
be lonely.

Isn't there anyone
who can love me?

I raise crops,
I feed the animals.
After a while
living becomes unbearable.
Nothing can fill
my emptiness.

Drowning in my
emotions,
without forethought,

MARDA

*I take the axe
with which I killed
my mother.
I bury it in my heart,
wrenching its bloody blade
from my mangled body,
only to bury the axe
in my heart
again.
Many times.
An agonizing
death.*

*I died
as I lived.*

*In the agony
of self-hatred.*

*Up there in the
heavens,
when I look back
on my life,
I clearly see
my cowardice.
I didn't embrace
life.
I hid from life,
behind the revulsion
of others
for me.*

*Can I rectify
such cowardice
when I return?*

*I fear I might forget—
it may be
too painful to remember.
Yet I know
I cannot continue
in that agony
of self-delusion.*

*"God!
If You exist,
help me.
Enlighten me.*

*"Do not allow
me to
waste
another
life!"*

Marda stopped speaking. Her silence seemed interminable. Finally she moved. She rose from the bed and looked above her, focusing on an energy that was invisible but, in her perception, clearly elevated.

Filled with fury, Marda screamed: "Who are you, Mary, to give me such information? Yes, I resemble him. But even though he's a killer-hulk, I don't want to separate from him. If this is my male energy, so what?

"Furthermore, I've been lying to myself and others about wanting to be a playwright. I'm a worker like him. I dress in workers' clothes like him. I'm more comfortable in these clothes than in frilly, feminine clothes. I prefer his kind of clothing even though I'm an executive. It's honest work, hard work!

"So fucking what if I'm not a playwright? That was a fantasy I concocted after I left college so I could feel separate from them. I was ashamed of them, of my background, all of it.

"Who are you, Mary? A part of my sick imagination? Leave me alone! I'm sorry I asked you to help me! I won't let go of Bruno. Yeah, that's my father's name. Never wanted to mention it before, because I was ashamed of him. Well, I'm not anymore. I love him—weird as he is, the hulk he is. I guess that means I won't let go of the reflected parts of him, either. So what if that means I will stay a victim?"

Her face was red with great anger. It was an intense rage, such as I had never seen before. She dressed, said she was leaving—would see me the following week. For right now, she'd had enough.

I opened my mouth to convince Marda to stay, to work out her difficulties about Mary. I had learned that it is unwise to leave a session in such an unresolved state. Before I could utter a word, however, Marda had thrown her fee for the session on my desk and raced out of the office.

Shaky and unsettled, I breathed consciously, calming my energy for my next patient.

12

Marda's Wake-up Call

Marda did not appear for her next session. I received a letter from her a few days after her scheduled appointment, from a hospital in northern Vermont. She'd had an automobile accident.

Dear Anneliese:
    Here I am, my right leg in a cast, suspended in the air by a pulley. My back is in traction. I'm immobilized and wonder if all those who have called me "beautiful" would consider me beautiful now. Otherwise, I'm physically okay.
    My friend, Ellen, and I were heading for Vermont on the thruway when the car suddenly skidded, veering to the other side of the road, where cars were traveling at least sixty-five miles an hour. I remember the ground coming toward me as I looked out of the left side window. I remember thinking that if we kept going I would be crushed.
    The car miraculously stopped, falling over on its left side. However, nine cars behind us went off the road or ran into one another. Fortunately, I was the only one hurt.
    I remember as the car rolled on its side, seeing a huge hand come down on my right side from behind to whack me. This was

a very powerful image, which has stayed with me, but one which I don't understand.

Is this accident the result of leaving your session enraged, unwilling to let go of my father, unwilling to listen to my higher voice, unwilling to face who I really am? Is the image of the hand the hand of God? I keep going over the scene with insane repetition. I've become involved in an obsessive litany which I can't stop. I fear I'm going crazy.

> The car I drove went out
> of control. It flew into the
> air. It turned over. It hit
> the ground hard, hard, hard.
> It's broken, the roof is crushed,
> the windshield gone. I flew. I
> hit hard. Nine cars were
> involved.
>
> I want to fly away. Fly back.
> I call for You and I hit hard.
> Hit the ground hard. I'm a
> killer, a sneak. I'm a girl.
> I'm a goy.
> I feel my chest open.
> God's hand is there.
> Why?
> Why do You want to save me?
> Why?
> Why now?

I want the litany to stop, but it feels as though it and I are on a carousel that's run out of control. I feel I'm on the verge of

MARDA

losing my hold on reality. Out of desperation I called to Mary to help me.

And this—if I'm *not* crazy—was Mary's answer.

> *Child of ours,*
> *resistant child,*
> *insistently confused:*
>
> *"Wake up!" we say.*
> *"You're one of us.*
> *Respect what we*
> *tell you."*
>
> *How much longer*
> *shall we be patient,*
> *knocking on your*
> *soul's door?*
>
> *This accident*
> *is a wake-up call.*
> *Pay attention!*
> *Do not ignore us.*
>
> *Your father is not*
> *your love.*
>
> *God is!*
>
> *Why do you forget*
> *your father's*
> *distorted acts,*
> *which wed you to*
> *him?*

*Enraged at God,
our obstinate Marda?*

*Desire change
and the answers
will be revealed.*

Anneliese, I wait impatiently to get out of the cast and traction to see you again.

My love to you,
Marda

13

The Initial Layer

Two months passed before I saw Marda again. She was still walking with a cane. Her right leg was not mending as quickly as she had expected. Her back had healed.

Her psyche, however, was in an uproar. She took her usual place opposite me. Her hands were busy folding and refolding. It was a more gentle variation of her hand-clasping gesture. She looked at me and looked away. Her lips began to tremble, her body shook. She tried to stay in control, but the dam burst.

Marda sobbed and sobbed. Her tears were the stored tears of a lifetime of agony. I have never seen so much pain emerge at once; it came from the center of her abdomen, flooding her heart, which appeared to be breaking, and to her face and eyes. I did not move toward her until it subsided.

But she still kept me at a distance. As if I were her confessor, she told me, "In the hospital, I felt I was going crazy. I implored God to hear me, to be there for me. Yes, I called on Him, or I would have gone out of my mind."

"I believe you, Marda," I said reassuringly. "Did you get a response?"

"Yes," she answered, a radiant smile coming to her lips. "He said:

> *Do you have eyes to see me?*
> *Do you have ears to hear me?*

> *Do you have lips to call my*
> *name?*
> *Do you have hands to do*
> *my work?*

"I answered:

> I've been saying,
> No! No! No!
> You gave me special hands
> with which I do my
> laborer's work.
> To that I've said,
> No! No! No!
>
> I'm strong and big.
> I've found love and help
> to nurture my acceptance
> of truth.
> I don't want to deny
> You anymore.
>
> Forgive me, God.
> Forgive my trespasses
> against You.
> I want to come to You.
> No longer reject You."

She reached her arms out to me. I embraced her with great warmth. She had made a giant leap as a result of her accident. I admired her for her determination to move out of her male victimization.

But I knew her fixation on her father still needed clarification.

"Marda, will you go down to the buried truth?"

"Yes," she said emphatically. "I must."

I asked her if she wanted to probe further. She gave me an emphatic yes.

She lay on the bed. I palpated her chest more deeply, encouraging imagery that pertained to other lives and other selves. She encountered lives in which she was in denial of life, obstinate, willfully rejecting herself, others, and God. She became aware of the choices she had made to split off from reality, to insanely isolate herself from life and humanity. She became aware of how she created evil behavior through her separation from herself and living life. She became aware of how her unconsciousness created more unconsciousness and more evil. She became aware of how bogged down with guilt her psyche became from all her denial. "Enough!" Marda screamed as she encountered herself. "Enough! Enough! Enough!"

I smiled to myself, filled with delight as I continued to palpate her chest and asked her to concentrate on her heart. I encouraged her to focus deeply into her heart.

She unexpectedly raised her index finger into the air and exclaimed with amazement, "It's like a pinpoint. It feels like the first connection to anything. I'm at the beginning of time." She was rapt—fascinated. "I see a compartment that resembles a beehive. It's occupied by a soul. It's hiding, hiding from the angels, hiding from everything. This soul is either hiding or peevishly whining. When I look around, there are many other souls in compartments that look like beehives. It's a pretty busy place."

"Look very carefully at the soul. Feel its vibration," I suggested.

Marda paused, then broke into unrestrained laughter. "That soul is me! I'm like a blob of protoplasm! I'm encased in a stiff, tight aura! The stiffness reminds me of Bruno, my father. What a sight! No wonder I've been referring to him and me as 'golems.' What a case I am! How I resent living, or movement, or change! I just want to stay mummified in my beehive compartment."

"Go more deeply into this layer to discover the basis of your resistance to living," I directed, excited by her probing, hoping she would find the reasons for her transgressions—not only against herself and men, but also against God.

"I'm in the firmament, restless, always looking, looking for God. Why isn't He with me? Why are we separate from each other? Why is He always so busy? I whine and sulk, 'He's mine, mine, nobody else's, but mine.'"

Marda became sad and perplexed.

"Then He threw me out,

> Out of His kingdom—
> down to Earth.
>
> Up there,
> He became impatient;
> I followed Him
> like a child—
> wanting to sit
> in His lap—
> for Him to be
> all mine.
>
> I was always
> under Him,
> around Him,
> on top, inside,
> outside.
>
> 'I want to be like You.'
> He said:
> 'You are you.
> Be you.
> I am who I am.
> You are you.
> Be it.'

The war began.
Not His—
mine,
and mine alone.

'You don't want me?
I'll fight You
all the way.
You are no longer my God.
My god will be men.

'Men became gods
for me.
Because
I'm angry at
You,
God.'

"Men became gods, because I'm angry at You, God," repeated Marda. "This is a revelation! I might have had to search forever for a normal male energy if I hadn't discovered this truth."

She repeated the sentence. "Men became gods, because I'm angry at You, God. And the sexual intimacy with you, Father, didn't repel me because I had rejected God and made you, Bruno, into a god."

Nothing more needed to be said. I was silently ecstatic. Marda had received the answer to her riddle, as Mary had predicted.

God,
let me come home
again.

Marda prayed, her beautiful face exalted with angelic humility.

I hear you, my child.
Cleanse and purify.
Pray for your redemption.
Praise me!
Your intent will be
heard.

Marda was on the first rung of the ladder, the ladder to ascension.

14

Marda's Resolve

I'm on my way.
Nothing is going to
stop me.
I'm stepping on the
first rung of the ladder.
And you down there,
fiery dragon,
watch out.
I'm leaving you
far behind.

Your flaming breath
becomes a harmless memory
of the time there was
before this time,
only one of all
the memories
that trickle
back into God's records,
which He keeps for all

humankind,
so that we may know
our own healing.

The pages are empty.
I'll keep them spotless.
I ascend,
chastened,
wiser.

Now,
God,
worthier of
Your
love.

Part Two

Christopher

15

The Soul of Christopher

Oh dear, dear, dear!
I thought it would be
quiet here.
I must have serenity,
I must have peace.
Otherwise,
I'm uncontained.

What is that commotion
not far from here?
A rancorous soul,
so violent, so unesthetic.
A disagreeable sight
to behold.

The angel follows it.
What shall I do?
Stay inside my compartment?
I'll read, I'll think,
I'll not be upset.
This too shall pass, I hope.

*The commotion has stopped,
thank God.
Excuse me, Lord,
but it's a way of speaking.
I want You to love me.
I'll behave.
Nothing should disturb
our harmony.*

*Quiet, sweet quiet.
So much better!
I can think, feel—
thinking is more
dignified.*

*Where was I when
hell erupted?
Yes!
How shall I spend my
life up here?
I'll be in this place a
long, long time,
respite from Earth.
I was good down there,
so very good—
death came unexpectedly.*

*The angel approaches.
He wants to converse.
I'll sit at the edge of
my compartment.
I'll wave.
He waves back.
It will be delightful*

*to speak with him,
an angel of stature.*

*He approaches.
He gestures with his
silvery net.
"Oh no," I say, "not that,
not yet."*

*I turn my back.
No,
I must be polite.
"Good morning, Angel
of Destiny.
Let's chat."*

*He stands, confused.
No one has ever befriended
him,
the inquisitor of the
firmament.
I repeat,
"Good morning, friend."
The angel relaxes and
considers entering.*

*"You're inviting me in?"
the angel asks,
incredulous.
"Come in," I say.
"We'll sit and chat
until we get tired.
Then rest, sleep, peace."*

*The angel is still surprised
but willingly enters.
We speak about the last
soul's departure.
"So obstreperous," I say.
"Your job is difficult."*

*"Correct!" says the angel,
tears coming to his eyes.
"You do understand my
frustration?
You'll come willingly, then?"
He smiles as he looks at me.*

*I sputter, but veil my
consternation.
I bow.
"If this be your desire."*

*"Follow me," says the
angel.
I follow, though stunned.
The Sages at the Council
are beatific.
They heard how I had
volunteered.*

*"This soul is going to be a male,"
they pronounce.
"A male," I repeat stoically.
Then off we go to the
departure depot.*

*We enter the silvery net
and sail out of the firmament,
quietly.*

*The Angel of Destiny
smiles lovingly at me.
I want to protest
my fate.
But to do so
would grieve my friend.
I do not wish to make
the angels weep.*

*We arrive on Earth.
A male and female are
copulating.
I look on, thinking,
"How exhausting.
I suppose in a few years
to do this will be my fate."*

*The angel invites me to step
out of the net, ready to place
me into the woman's womb.
I wave to the angel;
he waves back, saying,
"I'll see you shortly."*

*I adjust to an antiseptic womb.
The man's weight rests heavily
on her belly.
It's tight, cramped and frigid
in here.*

*I thought people were hot and
sweaty
when they copulated.*

*What is she doing?
She's reading now.
He has fallen asleep beside her.
She's a student of medicine;
he too is in medicine.*

*Lord! excuse me,
but—
let these nine months
pass swiftly.*

16

Our First Encounter

Christopher, a professional dancer of forty-three, sat stiffly in the chair opposite mine. He scrutinized me and my office. He smiled graciously, but his look was hungry and emaciated.

He told me he'd had four years of Bioenergetic therapy with another therapist, a male, but still found himself unable to commit to a woman. He chuckled at first, as though pleased with himself, but when he became aware of his chuckle he turned deathly serious, telling me that he was truly upset about this fact.

Margaret, who was his lover, also danced in his dance company. She loved him deeply but he could not return her love and, after being involved with her for four years, remained unclear about her. He had enough insight into himself to understand that he had either blocked his feelings toward her or simply did not feel enough for her to establish a permanent relationship. In the meantime, however, he was also sexually involved with another woman, who occasionally danced in his company as a principal dancer.

I noticed that this confession made him squirm in his chair. "I feel awful about such deceit. It's not the first time I've been sexually engaged with another woman while in a committed relationship, but I can't get a handle on the matter. At some point I become overwhelmed by guilt, the way I feel now telling you about it. Maybe it's because I'm confessing about this to a woman. Maybe it's because I just can't tolerate the lie anymore. I'm not sure. I need your help."

"I can see you're truly in pain. Who is the other woman? When do you see each other?" I asked.

"Lorraine is her name. We all dance together. You can imagine what that scene is like. Secrecy and lies. I must admit it's exciting for a while, but then the complications of the situation become too bizarre. Of course Margaret doesn't know about Lorraine, but Lorraine is completely aware of Margaret's role in my life.

"Margaret is totally devoted to me and I like that, but sex is boring. At the beginning of our relationship there was a great deal of passion, but of late I'm just not interested. I question whether it's a lack of desire for her or due to my rigorous schedule.

"But on the other hand when I'm with Lorraine, who is a fiery free spirit, I can make love for hours even though we meet after long hours of rehearsing. I don't know. It's tearing me apart."

"Would the fact that you come to her in secret, that you don't have to be involved in commitment, have anything to do with your passion for Lorraine?" I asked.

"I've thought of that, and it makes sense to me for a little while, but then it all gets jumbled in my head. I'm sure of one thing, though. I can't conquer Lorraine the way I do Margaret. This makes me anxious and unsure of myself. But, it's all coming to a head, so to speak. Margaret wants a commitment from me and lately Lorraine is getting tired of the secrecy and is pressuring me to choose between them. That's why I'm here."

"You're really in turmoil and I empathize with you. We can talk endlessly about your problem, but let's look at your body to get a diagnosis; perhaps your body will shed some light on the problem. Get undressed and stand in front of the mirror."

He removed his clothing rapidly, accustomed as a dancer to doing this many times a day. He approached the mirror with confidence and seemed to look forward to what he would discover. Christopher observed himself with pleasure, seeing a handsome face, a well-built body, muscular legs and thighs, and well-shaped feet with high arches.

I wanted to impress upon him that the diagnosis that would follow was a product of my observing the armoring of his body, not the aesthetic aspects of it. I assured him of his physical appeal, but said that it was the armoring that enslaved his psyche. He nodded.

I observed a contracted diaphragm, a paper-thin chest, and a thin, elongated neck that protruded beyond his chest and his large shoulders. He had long arms and large hands. When I placed him over the breathing stool to elicit breathing and corresponding emotions, he breathed mostly with his abdomen. There was little life from the umbilicus to the top of his head. His chest cavity was entirely flat, even concave, and from my many years' experience as a Bioenergetic therapist, I doubted that the heart center was energized at all.

I told Christopher that from my diagnosis, I felt he had had deep oral deprivation, starting from the beginning of his life. His body structure showed a lack of nurturing and a lack of bodily contact with his mother. His body seemed to scream out to be touched, held, looked at, paid attention to.

"You are deeply deprived, Christopher. No one was there to give you physical or emotional comfort. Such deprivation could create the neediness you feel in your present relationships."

He shrugged his shoulders.

"Where were your parents?"

"Absent," he responded with an edge of sadness. "But I don't perceive myself as needy. On the contrary, I'm quite self-sufficient and expert in controlling my needs."

I watched as he became aloof. He chuckled a little while kneading his fingers and began making a circular movement with the upper part of his body. It was as though by this gesture, subtle and almost imperceptible, he were dodging my comments, dispersing them into the air.

My impression was that Christopher, like many other patients, had learned in early childhood to separate the thoughts in his head from the feelings in his body. Moving on from woman to woman and situation to situation, he had tucked himself away in his head and, living in this smallest portion of his being, eluded life. The dance provided an outlet for breathing and physical expression, but in a very abstract way. Human expression was not desirable; on the contrary, it was the antithesis of the avant-garde movement he belonged to artistically.

"We have a lot of work ahead of us." I told him, "We'll begin at our next session. Will you be ready?"

"Yes. It's too uncomfortable to stay where I am. I'll think about what you said and I look forward to seeing you next week."

As I watched Christopher leave, I felt he was like a puppet under the control of a puppeteer—his intellect. Between the head and the umbilicus was an empty space, while the head told the feet, legs, and pelvis what to do next. I wondered about his history. I wondered what could have robbed him so completely of life.

17

The Next Session—Robbed of Life

"I was alone, always alone. Who and where was this woman I called Mother? I think I felt alone even in the womb, never so alone as there, and when I emerged I was still alone. She felt like marble, smooth and cold. I wanted to dig into her, but couldn't. It was as though she were only an impenetrable surface. No matter how I tried to reach her with my hands and arms, I couldn't seem to touch her, to feel warmth. The space between us was empty, empty, empty and cold. I remember dropping my arms, feeling totally anguished, forlorn—I remember feeling banished, feeling the empty space grow more and more empty. There was nothing I could do."

Christopher, after our last session, had decided to write down his feelings about his mother's absence. While he was reading I watched his hands, the fingers curved like claws or clenched into fists, shaping and reshaping themselves. He himself was unconscious of what he was doing. I realized that such formations were the result of his unsatisfied impulses to touch his mother's breasts and body when he was an infant. Because she had most likely denied such contact, he had to rechoreograph these primal impulses into more acceptable gestures. Today, as he sat before me, they translated themselves into kneading and pulling on his fingers. Certainly such gestures would be more acceptable to society than claws or fists.

Christopher was feeling the impact of his mother's coldness. He became quiet. I felt his sadness. "When you speak from your feelings, you are real and touching. Continue reading what it was like to be near your mother."

"Do I dare breathe you in? When I do, I breathe in your emptiness, your fear, your self-hatred, your suspicion that your husband doesn't really love you. It was a cultural match—two medical students, brilliant, promising. Why shouldn't they come together? They're of the same religion, the same upper class. They have the same interests, the same profession. The world around them says they're well-matched; so they must be. They married and she gave birth to me, a son, Christopher.

"My father, the gynecologist, avid to make a name for himself in the community, to make money, a lot of money, avid for social rank and prestige. He wasn't truly a kind, loving person, but a man frustrated and angry at women and at life. My father, who rode horses and beat them until they dropped from exhaustion or pain. My father, who wanted me to do the same. When I turned away and vomited when he bridled them so brutally that they bled from their mouths, my father, the gynecologist, sneered at my eight-year-old sensitivity and bridled the horses more fiercely. I ran away and threw myself on the ground sobbing. They were my last sobs. He had followed me and watched my heart-wrenching reaction to his brutality. 'My feminine sensitivity' is how he referred to it. My feminine sensitivity. What kind of a man would I become after such a display of weakness? This is what he asked as he stood with his crop pointing in my face."

There was a long silence. I saw his effort to control his heaving chest, which could have erupted into heavy breathing and deep sobbing, but he swallowed hard as he gained his usual control.

"Horrible, horrible, horrible, Christopher," I interjected, attempting to ease his embarrassment for his swallowed pain. "They were a unique couple."

"Were they ever," he responded, grateful for my feelings on the matter. "You would think that such cruelty would leak out on others, but on the contrary he was loved by his patients and my mother. She didn't want to interfere with his career and gave up hers, even though she'd received a medical degree. Can you believe this? She gave up her medical career and devoted her life to him?"

"He sounds like a self-involved but charismatic man."

"I guess so. I'm not clear about him, but I hope to get clarity. I remember that at the beginning of their marriage they went on camping trips by themselves. I guess they loved each other a great deal at that time. They didn't take us with them, but left us in the care of a cold, authoritarian, Prussian housekeeper. My sister and I were ecstatic when they returned; at least my parents' coldness and aloofness were familiar to us. My sister hates my mother and adores my father. I don't know what I feel toward either of my parents, or my sister."

"What do you feel right now about what you've read and said about your background?"

"It was a barren, desolate childhood. How did I survive? I guess Nature saved me. It's what kept me alive and feeling. I would play by myself in the woods for hours. I felt safe in the woods. I could feel myself in the ways I couldn't at home."

"How did you connect to yourself, Christopher?"

"As a little boy I had a lot of life in me. I had an athletic body. I loved it. I felt it. I lived in it. I played, played hard with the other boys of my age. They thought I was a 'cool kid.'" He chuckled as he recalled that time of his life. "But then I shut down and I wanted only to be alone."

"How old were you when you shut down?"

"Before ten—before the big drama occurred, which I'll tell you about in a moment. I shut down because there was no one I could relate to at home. When I connected to my mother, I felt her despair. When I connected to him, I felt his aloofness from me, from the family, even from his wife. What a self-involved man! You're right about him. But he was always beloved by his patients and the community. How ironic—a man who hates women, who is always invading their genital nature, the most intimate, precious part of themselves, is a man who hates women!"

"He lived from an appealing persona! Your mother bought it. Other women bought it."

"You're right. And then the pot boiled over. Everything went berserk. At ten, everything changed. He had found another woman, a friend of the family. Eventually he married her and was ruled subtly by her. My mother gained custody of us. She became utterly depressed and even more inaccessible. I went into the woods more often. I played by myself. I spoke to Nature. I was so alone. It took her two years to speak to us again. *Two years to speak to her children.*"

"That is utterly shocking," I interrupted, unable to restrain myself.

"I'm glad you're telling me so. It's important to have someone else's reactions; otherwise, I'm not sure I'm exaggerating the horror of my early life. This will shock you even more, but when she finally spoke to us, she never mentioned his name nor his lover's, her former friend. It was passed over like skipping important pages in a book. After she finally rejoined her children, I became her little gentleman, guided by her intellect, feeling her scorn if I dissatisfied her. None of it had warmth, none of it had love."

18

The Next Time

The next time for a session came four weeks later. Christopher arrived looking lost. He sat in his usual chair, facing me, but he was totally disconnected from his body, existing primarily in his head. He massaged his fingers as though he were obsessed. I noticed that the upper part of his body was tilted back, behind his umbilicus. This signified to me that his psyche was screaming to avoid all reality.

In this state he did not wish to be scrutinized by me and, most of all, he did not wish to be in the session. Nevertheless he smiled graciously from his divided self, at the same time chuckling nervously.

When I commented on the fact that the last session had been one of great release for him, he suddenly relaxed in his chair. His upper torso assumed a vertical position, joining the lower part of his body below his navel. As he felt the change in his body, a corresponding change seemed to occur in his psyche. I was witness to an astonishing transformation in a matter of seconds as he returned to the self I had become acquainted with. He released his fingers and, as he did so, shared with me the following experience:

"You're right. I did have a catharsis in the last session with you. It was the first time I felt good about spilling my guts to someone. Ordinarily I'm so much in control. But it didn't last long. In a short period of time I felt as if it had never happened."

"What happened to your good feelings?"

"When I arrived home, I received a message from my sister in California that I was needed urgently. This meant I had to have contact with my mother, which means I go into another gear—one of even less feeling than usual. My sister told me that the house in which both of us had lived all of our lives had been sold. My eighty-year-old mother needed to empty it of her possessions and move to a residence for the elderly."

"Not a small undertaking in a matter of a week," I said, remembering a similar situation in my own life. Christopher chuckled, happy he had an ally.

"My stoic mother hadn't bothered to let either of us know that a possible buyer of the property had given the real estate brokers a substantial deposit, sealing the contract and putting a limit on the time of her departure from the house. She must have been extremely ambivalent about leaving. Otherwise, she would have been more considerate and given us ampler notice. As it was, I had to cancel many professional activities in order to be available for her. However, I packed my bag immediately and found myself on the West Coast the next day."

I told Christopher that four weeks ago I had received a cryptic phone message from him canceling his next appointment, but with no explanation as to why. I explained that I had tried to reach him but was unsuccessful. I now realized that his immediate accessibility to his mother was typical of their interaction—an obedient, dutiful, though conflicted son.

"What happened when you arrived?"

"It was a dramatic time for me. The moment I stepped over the threshold of the house that had been my home for twenty-three years, I became mesmerized by the memories, the odors, and familiar vibrations. I was particularly struck by my mother's greeting. It was as I remembered it, an abstract greeting. She rushed to the door and, upon seeing me, stopped a few feet away. I had the distinct feeling that in this proximity, she contracted her body against whatever feelings she had and stuffed them into her head. Instead of a normal hug, a handshake, or an embrace, she became totally involved in questioning me about the length of the trip, its comfort or lack of comfort, and whether or not the airline hostesses had been courteous. We had no physical contact as she led me from the entry of the house into the interior.

"I felt some relief from my mother's coldness when my sister came galloping toward me and gave me a sisterly hug. I felt the tension that had been building up in me relieved by this hug and by her loudly expressed gratitude that I had, on such short notice, come to help. My mother, within earshot of that comment, became huffy and left the room. I recognized the old warfare between my sister and my mother and stiffened up against it. My sister ignored my mother's exit and began talking to me about the practical problems involved with packing and moving. Once again I was the object of both my sister's commandeering manner and my mother's forceful yet unexpressed demands on me. As I lay in bed that night, I noticed that I had, after only a few hours in the house of my birth, become a robot."

"Christopher, what you are telling me is extremely important and I'm totally involved in it, but I need to point out that you're not breathing. I want to hear all of your experience, but slow down. Breathe and feel what you're saying. Think that you are eating a wonderful, tasty meal and that you are savoring every morsel you put into your mouth."

"Okay. I'll try," he responded. "Packing . . . and . . . moving . . . became . . . our . . . main . . . activity. I began to see . . . that my mother . . . was being forced . . . to realize she . . . was no longer a staunch, independent . . . survivor."

"That's better!" I interrupted. "Try to feel and think at the same time."

"Whenever . . . my sister was . . . around, my mother . . . would continually revert . . . to her customary scornful state. My sister . . . stormed around the house, silently enraged . . . at my mother's insistence that all things . . . be done immediately and done her way. From my perspective . . . this was horribly unfair, since it was my sister . . . who had to complete the work . . . in only a few days."

Christopher stopped speaking. He was exasperated. "I can't tell you about my experience in any other way than in my way. So if you want to hear about it, please back off."

"You're right," I said. "I'm making you too self-conscious. Continue with your thoughts, but do try to connect feelingly in whatever way you can to what you are saying. And most important, breathe!"

"I'll try!"

He became comfortable again with his delivery. Soon he was speaking at a rapid pace. He reminded me of a locomotive that had to make up for lost time. I no longer interrupted.

"My mother was not oblivious to my sister's silent storming. She looked at me from time to time, expecting commiseration from her obedient son, but this time I didn't give it to her. Instead, I looked away. This was a gigantic step for me. I know it was only a tiny, reticent gesture on my part, considering what my mother's cruel behavior toward my sister really deserved. I was afraid, though, that I'd now get a dose of the coldness that was so familiar to me, so I went into my head and stayed there.

"In this fortress, I did the very thing I'd been trying not to do—colluding with my mother against my sister. My mother and I exist solely and exclusively in our heads and are split off from our bodies, so we related as we always had."

"Breathe, Christopher!"

"I am!" he shouted at me. "I am!"

He was again exasperated and fighting me to remain in his head. I gave up, knowing we would be working on this issue in depth as his therapy evolved. He was angered, but frightened to express himself in such a belligerent way to his therapist. He just wanted to go on with his story, which, in itself, was a catharsis for him. Once again I kept quiet.

"We worked on the packing for several days. In the late afternoons, I walked in the woods. I said a painful, feeling farewell to every blade of grass, every tree, every favorite haunt I'd had since childhood. I wanted to cry, but couldn't. I knew I would want to die if the suppressed feelings of that time were to surface. So I held myself in check as usual.

"After the move was completed, my sister returned to her family and I stayed with my mother for another day. She settled into her apartment at the residence for the elderly, stoically surrendering herself to a new existence. She recalled some conversations with friends long ago. I noticed that she told me her stories in a strange, confidential manner. I had the impression that I was the focus of her thinking. This idea shocked me. For the first time in my life, it occurred to me that she considered me her confidante, if not her lover or husband.

"I finally left. Again we had no physical contact. There was an abundance of insinuated love, however, which made me wish to vomit."

Christopher, upon hearing himself voice his own strong reactions to his mother, became abashed and perplexed. What was happening to him? Had he lost control of himself? When he began to knead his fingers, I seized the moment to push him to another psychological place.

"Repeat the phrase," I said quickly. "'Mother, I want to vomit you out.' Imagine her inside you. Do whatever is necessary to get her out of you."

He looked at me incredulously. "I couldn't do such a disgusting thing!"

I insisted.

He muttered repeatedly, "Mother, I wish to vomit you out! Get out of me!" He tried to vomit her out even though his esthetics were deeply offended. After many attempts, he became involved in powerful imagery related to their interaction. He screamed, "I can't release myself from her. I see our bodies intertwined, melded together. We're like Siamese twins. I try to separate from her but she's insidious in her grasp of me."

I suggested that Christopher pull her off him, even if it meant tearing her from his body. Christopher pulled and pushed the imaginary body of his mother away from him, but after he did so for a short period, his arms became limp. He moaned defeatedly, "I don't have the energy. It's left my body. I can't get her off me. I feel lifeless."

Christopher now understood for the first time in his life that he did not wish to get away from her. He addressed her in a squeaky, high-pitched voice: "I don't want to push you away, Mother. You're like dry ice, but you're all I've got. You're an intellectual robot, but you're mine. If I let go of you, I'll have no one to emulate. My father hated me. He thought I was a sissy. You at least talked to me. You came to my concerts. I've got to have someone, and you're embedded inside me. Without you, I'll be even lonelier than I've been all my life. I can't let go of you. I don't want to let go of you, yet."

Christopher had grabbed his imaginary mother and held her close to his chest. When he became conscious of his gesture, he quickly loosed the imaginary body and pushed it away. He pleaded with her sadly. "Get away. I can't hold you up, too, as well as myself. It's you who make me so ambivalent about women. Don't look at me in your insinuating way. I don't want you. I don't want to be your lover. I'm glad you never touched me. I'm glad I didn't have to embrace you ever, especially on that last trip. Your stale, odorless, unoccupied body frightens me and repulses me. Let go of me."

He hung his head as he sat in his chair, defeated. The experience had been too much for him. Slowly, out of habit, he returned to his neutral, cerebral place. Here, he was not torn apart by his ambivalence. Moment by moment he regained his familiar composure. He looked at me from his disconnected, controlled self, smiling his composed, meaningless smile.

I was astonished at how quickly he was thrown back to his former self. Seeing his unconscious effort to reestablish the rigid self, I shouted: "Freeze, Christopher! Stay exactly in the body language you have."

He did as I said. He felt his breathlessness, his rigidity. He cried out: "Oh, God, what have they done to me? Why did You let them do it? Why did I let it happen? Who am I? I'm possessed by my mother. How can I belong to anyone else when she exists so strongly inside me? How can I belong to myself?"

He cried gently while he rocked his body back and forth at the edge of his chair, mumbling, "Poor little lonely Christopher." He caught himself in this vulnerable state and quickly wiped the tears from his eyes. I took his hands and looked at him with compassion. He smiled a grateful smile.

Christopher left the office that day a little more connected to his feelings—feelings that were difficult to bear; feelings that defined an emerging self, a self sealed in a dry, stuck body.

I understood that there were miles to go before that self would be touched again, before he could remain fully with his feelings.

19

Margaret—Ambivalence

In subsequent sessions, I urged Christopher to put his mother's image on the bed, as is done in the Bioenergetic modality, and to explore his real feelings toward her. This proved to be a most revealing, grounded experience for him. He had never allowed himself to feel this kind of honesty toward her. Instead, he had put her on a pinnacle devoid of reality. It was with her on this inaccessible height that he had related to her and she to him. Exchanges of real feelings were not possible for either of them, since neither was willing to see the other, except as images that fed their fantasies.

As Christopher delved into the effects her emotional unavailability had had on him, he saw her as a "stupid bitch" with no guts and no ability to face life, as someone who felt no responsibility toward anyone but herself. He became aware of her manipulative nature, which had made him her captive. He began to understand how emotionally deprived he always had been and how he used this deprivation to manipulate and enslave other women.

In session after session, Christopher became clearer about his mother. At the height of his clarity, he confessed to Margaret about his relationship with Lorraine. He no longer wanted to live deceitfully nor in a state of ambivalence. Margaret, his lover of four years, was devastated and asked to join him in his next session. Christopher was fearful but relieved that he would no longer have to carry such a weighty secret by himself. I was happy that he had finally become discontented with his dishonesty. I readily consented.

I found Margaret to be a passive, thin, attractive young woman, thirteen years younger than Christopher. She sat in a chair opposite me, beside Christopher. She said little after our introduction and waited for him to speak. He introduced the topic of his ambivalence toward her. He was concerned about their lack of communication. Should they separate?

As he said this, Margaret moved in her chair as though she wanted to leave the room. Instead, she swallowed what she was feeling and again sat like an obedient waif.

"Margaret," I asked, looking at her directly, "what do you feel about Christopher's unclear feelings toward you?"

She writhed in her chair, looked at him, looked at me, then planted her feet on the ground and banged her fists on her knees as she told him, "I'm sick of it! Sick of it! Do you hear, Christopher? I'm sick of your ambivalence." She hesitated for a moment, seeing that Christopher was jolted, but that at the same time he was excited by her directness.

I suggested that she work through her feelings in the Bioenergetic fashion by going to the bed with Christopher, where she could express her anger fully rather than hurt herself by pummeling her knees. Margaret was fearful, but her desperation to achieve clarity about his behavior overrode even the fear she was feeling. I placed the two of them at the ends of the bed, facing one another.

At the bed Margaret picked up the racquet and examined it. She had seen Christopher release his anger on the bed at various times since they had known one another. Intuitively she held the racquet over her head and behind her shoulders, ready to express herself. In this position she suddenly hesitated, looking at Christopher apprehensively, wondering if she dared say what she felt. She looked like a gambler about to take the ultimate risk.

Once Margaret had made her decision, however, she gained confidence and momentum, unleashing what seemed to be four years' worth of stored-up frustration. She screamed at Christopher: "You betrayed me with

Lorraine! How could you do something so evil? I'll leave you if you don't give her up. You don't tell me your feelings, and yet you complain that I don't tell you mine. You treat me like a slave, not only in our personal life but in your dance company. I don't know why I stay with you. Whenever I ask you for something, like having sex, you fall asleep or are outraged at the demand. I give you what you want, but you're a stillborn when it comes to giving back. You're a bore a good part of the time, with your constant withdrawal when you don't get exactly what you want."

Christopher listened. He was flabbergasted at her lucidity and her anger. He stood at his end of the bed, dumbfounded. She had never spoken to him in such a manner; he was suddenly afraid to lose her, a feeling that was new and baffling.

"React, Christopher, react," I instructed. "Not from your head but from your feelings. Express what you feel, no matter how irrational it might be. Don't be afraid. They're your feelings."

He stood for a long time, numb and bewildered, until he finally yelled: "I'll do what I want! Don't tell me what to do. I'll sleep with whomever I please. Get your hands off me and keep them off. I'll live my life my way, not yours. You need me too much and I don't want to give to you. Find your own life and live it. Don't depend on me to provide you with energy. Keep your hands off."

Margaret looked at him and her exasperation grew into total rage. She screamed back: "If that's what you feel about me then take a walk! You're a bottomless pit. What I've given you is wasted. You'll never be satisfied. Anyway, I don't want a sexually rigidified ghost." She threw the racquet on the bed and said that she was leaving.

I went to her, took her hands in mine, and assured her she had been very courageous to tell Christopher what she felt. I then asked both of them to sit on the bed next to each other. They sat apart and waited for me to speak.

"The energy between you is stale, boring, and unmoving," I explained. "Why? Because neither of you expresses your negative feelings to the other. These feelings need to be sorted out because they relate not only to the both of you but to your parents as well. Until you are more conscious about whom they belong to, you will stay in a morass of unconsciousness and the relationship will become deadlocked.

"You're new to therapy, Margaret, but understand that the psyche's tendency is to 'paste' reactions belonging to our parents onto not only a partner but onto others as well. These reactions are feelings that could not be expressed in childhood. They are reactions that get stored in the psyche and are constantly being triggered by what another person does to us. We are usually completely unconscious of the triggering. It is therefore our responsibility to make ourselves aware of where our reactions began.

"For example, Margaret, sort out which of the feelings you expressed earlier belong to Christopher and which belong to your parents."

"Feeling like a slave to Christopher is a familiar feeling," she offered quickly. "I guess it originates from my family. I love Christopher deeply and so I want to give to him. But, he's insatiable with his needs. The more he gets, the more he wants."

"Can you connect all these insights to your background?" I asked.

It took little time for Margaret to make an important connection.

"When I was growing up, I got almost nothing from my parents, which made me behave like a beggar waiting for them to recognize me. It seems that I'm in a parallel situation with Christopher, because he, like them, is also emotionally stingy."

"How does this affect you?"

Without hesitation she said, "I see now that this triggers me into slavelike behavior with all of them. Currently with Christopher. What a mess!"

"You're very quick to understand, Margaret," I said sincerely.

"It's time to be wiser," she said, anxious to continue. "I wonder if I'm staying in this relationship because no matter how little Christopher gives me, it's more than I got from my parents. Once again I've put myself into a deprived situation and I just don't say anything."

At this point Margaret looked at me intensely. I asked her what she wanted to do.

Not looking at Christopher, she said clearly, "I'll no longer tolerate his withdrawn, cold behavior. And most important of all, I'll no longer accept another woman as part of the relationship, and he'd better choose now."

Margaret was able to understand that with so little generosity in her childhood, she had become passive and undemanding. She said that she was astonished at how much rage had built up in her psyche about her deprivation. In a state of disbelief, she exclaimed, "I would never have thought that venting these horrible feelings would make such an enormous difference in how I feel about myself right now. I feel good, clean, clear—like myself. It's amazing."

I turned to Christopher. He said that what he had expressed toward Margaret was totally about his mother. He realized that Margaret's neediness did get on his nerves, but that the hostility it incited basically belonged to his mother.

"Margaret," said Christopher, "I'm sorry for having been abusive. I see now how alive you are and how much I've squashed your vitality. When I'm cold and self-indulgent, tell me so. Otherwise, I back off from you and blame you for all kinds of things. My mother was a needy, mute, vampire of a woman. When you become needy and mute, I can't separate the two of you. I want you to know that I've already given up Lorraine. I want you and me to go on together."

Margaret was moved by his decision. She sat closer to him. He held her hands and stroked her hair. She asked me what they could do to stop triggering each other.

"It's tricky, Margaret," I said. "Remember that your neediness sends Christopher into his head, where he plots and schemes on how to avoid you. This intense unavailability brings you into a state of needy helplessness. When you are both in such a place, you paw at each other like two helpless, blind animals wanting attention. If neither of you is aware of what you're projecting, the relationship dives into total unconsciousness and eventually sinks in its own trapped energy."

"We don't want to go on like this," they said, almost in unison.

"And I had better do my own work on myself," said Margaret, asking for an appointment.

I gave it to her and thanked her for her receptivity. I realized once again how growing consciousness is akin to God's light. I realized, too, that growing consciousness brings one ever closer to desiring ascension.

20

Victimization

Margaret and Christopher moved in together. They often met roadblocks in their relationship. She would become passive and needy because he acted cold, distant, and rejecting. In this state they stopped communicating and their household resembled a morgue.

Both understood from the work they had done in their first joint session with me that they had pasted their parents' images on the other. When they did not catch their negative transference toward the other, they submerged their feelings in a cavern of resentment, irrationality, and paralysis.

They resisted getting into a bogged-down relationship, however, by working intensely in individual and joint sessions and in an ongoing group of which they had become members. No longer were they content to let problematic issues pass them by, but addressed them quickly. In doing so they removed the patterns of behavior that had kept them stuck; their relationship gained clarity and momentum. Consciousness grew and a gradual freeing of their respective psyches ensued.

Two years passed while Christopher and Margaret were avidly engaged in self-discovery. Changes occurred, but Christopher, despite the progress he was making, remained ambivalent toward Margaret. Although more subtly than before, he continued to feel victimized by her and by any demand she made on him. He wallowed in persecution.

Margaret's sympathy for his familial neglect caused him to act out on her; her love for Christopher as well as her fear of assertion often dampened her objectivity. She humored him until he was satisfied, but he was relentless in his denial of her when she was not present unconditionally. It took all her strength to assert her indignation at such times, when she called him a bottomless, unappreciative brat. He would then sniff out other possibilities, other potential female candidates to fill his "bottomlessness." He never acted from this vindictive tendency, however, because he realized that Margaret would no longer tolerate another bout of infidelity.

Christopher leaned heavily on Margaret's female energy. During one of our group sessions, this imbalance became clear to me. It was his demanding interaction with Margaret that exposed his missing connection to his father, who had been emotionally absent, aloof, and disdainful all of his life. Christopher's male energy was therefore lacking, confused, and repressed. He experienced such lack as a gaping hole in his male energy. This lack kept him so unbalanced that even after years of therapy, he could not disengage himself from the female energy of his mother. His mother's energy allowed him to feel that someone was there for him and that he was not alone in the world.

During another group meeting, his need of a male image became crystallized. It happened indirectly, at a time when all of the group members were asked to express their feelings toward one of their parents. They were asked to physicalize their feelings and to accompany whatever movements emerged from their physicalizations with words. The room was buzzing with their portrayals. Christopher was deeply engrossed. I observed what he was doing.

He had again chosen his mother. He stuck out his tongue as though vomiting her out, then moved his body from side to side, screaming, "Yes! No! Yes! No! Get away! Come here! Get away! Come here!"

His ambivalence was absolutely clear. His body language revealed precisely how unequivocally he was stuck to his mother, Margaret, and all women. He looked at me forlornly as if to say, "So what? I know all this!"

I was challenged to push him on. I placed Leonard, an older member of the group, in front of him. Christopher scrutinized him and spoke without deliberation. "You were never interested in me at all. I've inherited your love of nature, but you didn't even know that about me. You hurt me very badly. You don't like your son to cry, but I'm crying now and I don't care if you don't like it. I missed you all the time. Where were you?"

Christopher's sobs were deep and anguished. He was, without question, immersed in his feelings.

"I didn't like being in the stables with the horses because of how you treated them. I only did it to be with you. Can't you let down and be simple? I love you for some good you didn't even know you had. You should be deeply sorry. Do you see who I am? Do you see who I am?"

Christopher looked longingly at Leonard, who held him as he cried deeply, letting go of the pain of not having had a father. He let go of the pain of feeling how deeply he lacked his own male energy, and how he had compensated for the imbalance in his nature by over involving himself with his mother. Leonard held Christopher for a long time and Christopher soaked in the simplicity and directness of the male strength.

Margaret went to comfort him, but he wanted to be held only by a man. He sat down next to Leonard, who clearly represented his father, holding Leonard's hands and kneading Leonard's fingers.

My impression was that Christopher wanted to be touched all over his body by those male hands, to feel their strength, their directness, a touch that might kindle in him his own male energy. My further impression was that Christopher was not only delighted by this newly discovered male strength, but felt contaminated by the female energy.

While he was feeling secure in his male imagery with Leonard, I asked a female group member to role-play by standing seductively before him. She reached toward Christopher enticingly. Without thought, he pushed her away. His rage erupted and was boundless. He threw her to the ground, screaming, "Die! Die! Die! I can't stand you!"

Christopher was bewildered by the intensity of his violent unconscious impulses toward his mother. He was pale with horror at the idea of having wished her dead. Nevertheless, he did not want to stop working.

He told us that another issue was gnawing at him. He returned to Leonard and picked up his hands. He said he needed to have the security of a man's hands in his own while he told us two dreams he had a few nights before.

He spoke nervously. "In the first dream, I see a pretty young man bending over, naked. I'm having sex with him, standing up, penetrating his anus. We don't know one another. I feel strange and entranced by the physical sensations and the wildness of it. In the second dream the same night, I take the semen from my ejaculation after masturbation and place it into another man's mouth. I feel totally satisfied by doing this."

Timidly, Christopher looked at some of the faces of the group members, embarrassed and frightened. In a soft voice he told us that since his ambivalence was so pervasive and since he had so much anger and confusion toward the woman and was so needy of male energy, he was afraid he might be a repressed homosexual.

His fear was palpable as he nestled closer and closer to Leonard. Christopher was waiting for a verdict. He nervously resumed kneading Leonard's fingers as he looked at the faces surrounding him. He seemed like a doomed man.

I sympathized with his sensitive state, but believed he should remain in that state while he worked in depth on his issue. I told him to role-play the two dreams.

"I believe you will learn a great deal from physicalizing your dreams, Christopher," I assured him, "because you will not be able to resort to your overused intellect and will therefore call upon your unconscious to give you the meaning of the two dream experiences. Being literal is not necessary; our imaginations are fertile. Getting emotionally involved with the setup of the dreams, however, will shed light on what your unconscious is trying to tell you."

He proceeded to activate the first dream. He imagined a male body before him. He pretended to penetrate the male's anus. As his sexuality got ignited, Christopher yelled out, "Now I've got you where I want you. I'm fucking you as you've fucked me all my life. How does it feel? You spanked my bare buttocks whenever you could, you sadistic maniac. You bridled my buttocks the way you bridled the horses. How does it feel, father, the beloved gynecologist? It hurts, doesn't it? Well, take the pain! I had to take the pain when you banged away at my buttocks and I was too little to fight back. Horrible beast of a man. What's your problem? What's your fucking problem?"

Christopher was breathing heavily. Once more he looked around the room at the faces of the members, then at me. He beamed like a man who had stepped out of hell.

Feeling visibly more powerful, he set up the action of his second dream. He again placed before him an imagined male figure. In his hands he had his own semen. He said, "I see you as a handsome, strong, integrated man. I bestow upon you my seed, my essence. From that essence I will be born. From that essence will emerge the male I am intrinsically, the male I always have been from the time of God's conception of me. I give this to you as we fuse to become my true male energy."

The room was silent. Tears came into some of the members' eyes.

Christopher took his place next to Leonard. His face was aglow. He wept unrestrainedly. At the same time, he looked around the room and then at me, grateful for his renewal. Nothing more needed to be said. The members flocked around him. He received their warmth, their comradeship, their understanding.

21

Victimization versus Reflectivism

Christopher came to his next session feeling good about the work he had done in the group. At the same time, however, he had an added attitude of delicacy, like a wounded bird. He wallowed in his woundedness. He complained about Margaret's impatience with his indulgent neediness and wondered if I too found him indulgent.

Here was the opportunity I had been waiting for to introduce him to the concept of Reflectivism.

"Christopher, you can go around and around blaming your parents for their injustices, but, in doing so, you remain a wounded victim—always espousing your pain, stuck in your victimization, in its negative energy. You become arrested in this state, blaming them and life for giving you a raw deal.

"In the beginning of analytical work, it is necessary to become conscious of the causes of the pain in one's life. It is important to become a warrior against the oppressors. But can you imagine, Christopher, remaining on such a treadmill forever? Can you imagine that, by continually blaming your parents, you will ever develop a real self? Margaret finds you boring and childish when you act like a victim. When you look inside yourself, can you find another Christopher besides the hurt, abandoned, manipulated Christopher?"

"Yes," he replied. "He's the one who dances, the one who loves nature. He's kind, sensitive. He's also cruel and manipulative. But I discount the cruelty and manipulativeness because I learned it from them. It's not me. How can it be me, when I was so neglected?"

"This will blow your socks off, Christopher, but perhaps you are cruel, manipulative, and cold like them because these qualities are not only in them, but in you as well."

"Me?" he asked dumbfounded. "How can that be? I was so oppressed!"

"Believe this or not, but you came into this life with those qualities lodged in your psyche. You chose your parents prenatally so you could learn this truth about yourself. You're a mirror reflection of them. If you are willing to accept this truth, you can move out of your victimized state into a fuller, more realistic vision of who you are."

"And how do you know that I came into this life with these qualities?" he asked, with a mixture of curiosity and skepticism.

"I believe all of us choose our parents before we are born in order to give us the right dimension for further growth," I answered quickly. "That is, if we wish to look beyond our victimized self."

"How?" he asked uneasily.

"You must expand your horizon about living. You must consider that we have all lived millions upon millions of lives, in which we have been male and female. We have been different races, been rich, poor, physically fit as well as physically unfit. We've sinned, been redeemed, sinned again, and rectified our mistakes until we achieved another consciousness. Our goal, though deeply buried, is ascension. To achieve ascension, we must look at ourselves in an expanded way, willing to face all aspects of ourselves, no matter how unsavory."

Christopher was thoughtful. "I don't want to remain a victim. I've become aware that whenever I pull this victim stunt with Margaret, I feel immediately good, but moments later I feel ashamed and want to kick myself. I used to apologize, but now Margaret pulls away from me in disgust and I feel like cringing in a corner, sucking my thumb. I feel like a spineless rag. This victim stuff comes upon me when I'm criticized by you or Margaret, or anyone I care about."

"Terrific, Christopher. You understand what I am doing. What else do you know about being a victim?"

"Well," he said delighted that he could expound his insights on the matter, "since I'm a victim par excellence, I know that playing it out has power. I know because I've used it successfully on all women, starting with my mother. Ironically, with her, I had to compete as to which one of us would get the other's attention. She won. Since I couldn't get it from her, I manipulated the other women."

We both laughed at his honesty.

"What a long way you've come," I said.

"What have I got to lose? I'd better let go of my 'case,' otherwise I'll never become me."

"Good for you! It seems that your work in the group was a real breakthrough experience. What else have you discovered?"

"It was a breakthrough! I got a glimpse of some degree of wholeness when I gave my semen to the imaginary man in my dream. Momentarily, I felt in truth. But I couldn't hold on to it. I'll remember the experience, though, knowing there can be more of the same. I don't want to be a victim anymore. I want more of me. If it means that I've been stuck like this in other lives, then let me look at them. I'm willing to look at the repulsive, appalling parts of me."

"Great! Let's do it!"

"Okay," he said, wondering if he wasn't being too cavalier. He noticed that his hands were shaking.

"But let's do it before I lose my courage."

22

Reflectivism: The Male Energy

Christopher lay on his back on the bed. His willingness to probe further warmed me. I instructed him to go into his imagination and write the words: ARROGANCE, CRUELTY, and SELF-INVOLVEMENT—his father's qualities—on a wall. When he had done so, I suggested he see the words emblazoned on this wall in purple and red. (Colors can impassion a person or be calming. Purple and red have a "breaking through" effect on the psyche, an effect that stimulates the imagination, bringing one to another dimension.)

Christopher imagined the words in these two colors and allowed himself to become mesmerized by all he saw inwardly: the words, the colors, and his desire to find another self. Slowly he broke through the adjectives and the imagined wall to another world.

He found himself in new territory, territory he could not control intellectually. He was submerged in his unconscious in a manner unfamiliar to him. When I asked him where he was, he said he was enveloped in darkness, where shapes and forms were emerging and receding. I urged him to grab hold of whatever shapes became visible and to concretize them.

"It's hard to choose. There are so many." After a long pause he said, "It feels as if a particular one is taking form over the others. The shape of a young man becomes clearer. It's getting even clearer. He's walking in a thick forest, wearing leather sandals and leather shorts, alone, with a small bundle of clothes in a sack. In his hands is a bow and arrow.

"I feel a kinship with him. He loves the woods. *I* love the woods. He loves being alone in the woods. *I* do too. He feels like me. *I* feel like *him*." There was a sudden shift in Christopher's consciousness. He became the character. "I've got to be careful. I've got to be wary. They might come for me. I can't be discovered. Otherwise, I'll be killed. Here's a tree. It's hollowed out—just right for my body. I'll sleep in it. I'm tired, so tired. Running, running all the time. No place is right for me. Nobody wants me. Nobody ever wanted me."

I'm twenty,
dark and strong.
I love animals,
the forest.
I hate humanity.

A man comes
into my woods.
He shouldn't be here.
No one should be here.
They're my woods.
I stalk and kill him,
mercilessly.
I eat his flesh
and take the money
from his purse.

I loathe you all,
all mankind.
You treated me
cruelly.

CHRISTOPHER

How did I get this way?
It started early.
I became an orphan
at ten years old.
My mother's friend
promised she'd
take care of me.
But she didn't
in the long run.
She gave me a corner
in her kitchen.

She never wanted
me there and told
me so.
At sixteen, I took
my bow and arrow
and whatever clothes
I had and left.

A farmer gave me
lodging in return
for feeding his animals.
I ate the slop they got
and soon turned into
one of them.

No human contact
came my way.
Soon I grunted
like the animals.
I was big, strong
and hairy—
so strong I almost

*killed the farmer's
son,
who threw a rock
at me.*

*I grunted, groaned,
and spat on the earth
as I lifted him from
the ground—
one hand on his back;
the other around his
neck.*

*He turned purple.
I laughed uproariously.
I dropped him just in time.
I took my clothes and
fled.*

*I like it in the woods.
When any man comes
near my habitat
I stalk, kill, and
steal from him.*

*Word gets out.
I'm a dangerous killer.
Those who venture
into my woods
never leave.
That makes me laugh.
I live like this
for at least five
years.*

CHRISTOPHER

*I'm safe
and feel secure.*

*In time
I become lonely.
I want to see others,
though I hate them.
I leave my woods,
taking refuge a distance
from the nearest town,
the town I'd fled from.*

*I shave, cut my hair,
look like a human.
I get more brazen.
I sit in the village square.
I eye the others—
but I'm always on the
alert.
Slowly I relax my guard.*

*People begin to nod
to me.
I feel less lonely.
I relax, even daydream
of a mate.
Suddenly I hear a shout
from a distance.*

*Before I'm aware,
I'm on the ground,
a burly body
on top of me.*

*I look into the face
of the farmer's son.
He spits and screams
like a wild man.
He bangs my head on
a rock.
I'm stupefied
and helpless.*

*Four others
who recognize me
from long ago
take me to a tree
and hang me by
my feet.*

*My arms wave
futilely in the air.
In time the blood
rushes to my head.
It bursts my veins.
I die a slow,
agonizing death.*

*It's over!
I'm dead at last—
No longer subject
to
man's
cruelty.*

Christopher lay on the bed, slowly regaining his contact with current reality. "What a story! I never would have believed that such a character was hiding inside me. I can't refute any of it. I don't kill people in this life, but sometimes while I'm walking on the streets of New York City, I have the distinct feeling that I want to kill anyone who might touch me accidentally, might look at me in a hateful way, or might simply be in my way. Deep down I hate people, don't want to be near them. I also feel they're beneath me."

"This must be a difficult realization for you. Have you ever been aware of your hatred toward humanity before?" I asked, totally supportive of his honesty.

"I've had inklings of it, but I never let it come to the surface. I'm really like my father: arrogant, self-involved, and cruel. No wonder I can't connect to others in a meaningful way. I relate to others cerebrally, that's all. As far as the dance is concerned, I don't give much of myself to the audience either, hiding behind meaningless abstraction. Yet I want them to applaud me after a concert. How can they? They must unconsciously pick up my disdain for them."

Christopher continued, devastated. "I'm a fraud, a big fraud." He turned his body to the wall and wept. "Oh, God! Help me! Help me out of this confusion. How much longer do I need to hide from myself? Where would I be without an inheritance? I wouldn't have made it! Thank you, God, for that at least."

I came to him and held his hand. "You are genuinely courageous to face these truths."

"I guess so," he answered, resigned. "They're difficult." He took many deep breaths, which seemed to give him courage. "These truths are hard to look at. I always thought the qualities of the man in the forest were only in my father. I see now how they're mine, too. If I've come to Earth to rectify, I might as well go all the way. I've nothing to lose. My male is exposed. I want to go on."

"I'm proud of you, Christopher. You're a fighter."

He was heartened.

"What's next, Anneliese? My mother's energy?"

"Exactly! It would be good to see how her qualities live in you."

"I suppose I've got to look at how I'm like her, a piranha like she is; otherwise, as I did with my father, I'll go on perceiving her as the piranha and me as the poor victim."

We hugged before he left my office. I was struck by the strength of his hug. It was no longer tentative or passive. His male energy was emerging.

23

Reflectivism: The Female Energy

Christopher arrived at my office, bewildered. He had received a telephone call from his mother on the West Coast telling him that his father had died. His father's present family surmised that he had been thrown from the horse he was riding on a steep, narrow, remote path. His foot had become caught in the stirrup, his body dragged for many miles as the horse ran at full speed back to the stables.

"What a horrible death!" I said to Christopher.

He was silent. After a while he told me that he had few reactions to his father's death. "The only thought that crosses my mind is a passage from the Bible: *As you cast your bread upon the water so it will return.* It was a horrible death. I hope he didn't have to suffer long. Overall, the strongest feeling I have is that I wish he could have been my daddy. But this was not our destiny. What I can do is learn from all of it and use whatever I learn to continue growing. Maybe one day I'll be able to forgive him. Right now, this is where I'm at. I'm sorry he had such a horrible death."

Christopher then took a number of deep breaths and said he was ready to get on with what we had been planning to do in this session.

"I can imagine what you're thinking," he added. "Well, the answer to your question is that I can take more. I'm long overdue for a rebirth. I'm ready to put *Mom* in order in my psyche. You don't want me to be lopsided, do you?"

His eyes twinkled. I saw a strength in him that was ever-growing.

I asked him if he recalled the adjectives he had used to describe his mother. "Do I ever!" he responded. *"Narcissistic! Aloof! Cruel!"*

I told him to picture these three words emblazoned in red and purple on a wall. He did so and was swiftly swept into the adjectives and the colors. His eyelids fluttered rapidly as his entry into another story began.

He wriggled his body when I asked him his gender. He said that it felt delicate and soft-skinned. After a short time examining his body, he spoke like an abstract dancer, whose descriptions were brief but pointed:

> *Pink, soft skin.*
> *Beautiful,*
> *blond,*
> *only twenty.*
> *A princess in a*
> *medieval castle.*
>
> *My parents' kingdom,*
> *of fear and rebellion.*
>
> *I hate the rabble.*
> *They smell,*
> *they breed like animals.*
> *Still, once a month,*
> *I walk among them.*
> *A symbol of their*
> *future queen—*
> *my parents' orders.*
>
> *I abhor this event.*
> *Loathe it.*
> *They hate me as*
> *I hate them.*

CHRISTOPHER

*They line the streets
and shout my name.
They do this under
penalty of death.*

*I walk among them,
smell their smells,
see their coarse faces.
A scented handkerchief
is at my nostrils,
preventing nausea
and the desire to
vomit on them.
They hate me, too.*

*"Mother, father.
Why do you do this
to me?
I abhor this event!
Why must it continue?"
No answer.*

*I'm in my bath,
cleansing my body
of their hateful feelings.
I'm beautiful,
so beautiful,
but oh,
so miserable.*

*Nothing excites me.
I'm on my veranda—
my section of the castle.
The sun is warm,*

the air is fresh.
Yet, I do nothing
but stare at the lands
that one day will be mine.
I sigh.
And return to nothingness.

A national holiday—
my birthday.
I must ride and walk
among the rabble.
A new gown for the
occasion.
To that I look forward.
I'll be more beautiful
than ever.
Damn the event.

On that day, I bathe
more luxuriantly.
My servants soap my body.
I'm aroused.
I clench my sexual areas
so tightly—
instead of a full release,
only a contracted howl
comes through.

To clench and strain
is the teaching of
the queen, my mother.
No sensation should be felt.
She gave birth to me
at an older age.

*No doubt she'd been
too contracted
for passionate loving
to take place.*

*My gown is ready.
I wear it like a queen.
"Rabble, look upon
this beautiful woman,
who will bring you
to your knees."*

*In my carriage,
drawn by eight horses.
I have a large supply
of scented handkerchiefs.
Each scent brings me delight
while I wave my hand to
those lining the streets.*

*All is going well,
I think.
They cheer loudly,
though mechanically.
I could fulfill my
role as their queen.*

*The carriage lurches.
The horses' legs are in
the air.
The soldiers bring them
to a halt.*

*A man shouts,
"Stop the carriage!"
A woman cries in horror.*

*The man takes from
underneath the horses' legs
the dead body of his
four-year-old son.*

*The body is raised
above the man's head.
He looks toward me—
"Murderer! Murderer!"
He rushes toward the
carriage.*

*"How dare he!"
I think,
my handkerchiefs at
my nostrils.
"Turn the carriage around,"
I scream.
"Race toward the castle."*

*"It's not my fault,
my fault!
Not my fault!"
The litany is incessant.
My parents put me to bed,
a servant watching over me.
"Not my fault,
my fault!
Not my fault!"*

CHRISTOPHER

*"Spare me another event
like this," I plead.
My parents smile.
"This is a small trial
in the life of a queen."*

*I sleep as though drugged.
In the morning when
I awaken
I feel tired, wishing
not to live.
I go to the veranda.
The sun's rays are vibrant.
I reach out my arms
to this body of warmth,
asking it to revive my spirit.*

*I hear a rustling of the
leaves.
I see the man whose
son had been killed.
I assume he came to beg
my pardon.*

*I remain standing with
outstretched arms.
He is poised with bow and arrow.
He shoots into my heart—
a heart so forlorn, so cold.*

*I drop to the ground—
dead.*

> *My body is found later.*
> *There is no trace of my assailant.*

Christopher remained with the body of the princess. He spoke to her. "Pathetic, neglected, unfeeling, cruel, narcissistic, aloof little girl. I'd like to warm you up, bring life into you. I'd like to bring life into myself, because you and I and my mother are the same. I've got to discard yours and Mom's energy from my system. Continuing to blame you, Mom, is futile. I'll have enough to do to change so much negativity in me. I can look at my own negative qualities and take responsibility for changing them. These qualities have kept me in despair, in isolation, in judgment of others, in avoidance of life. Margaret, why have you tolerated such an unloving nature as mine? I've given you nothing but crumbs."

I explained, "Had you chosen to remain a psychological victim, you would not have experienced this realization. You now have a clearer goal."

Christopher was pleased with himself and sweetly told me that he felt he'd had many transformations. I commented that he was clearer about his reflected selves, for which he should be proud.

"I accept them and want to work to change them. I now want to get a realistic sense of who my female and male selves really are. My first test will be Margaret. I want to give to her fully. I hope I can. I'll let you know in the next session what happens."

"You are on your way, Christopher. On your way to ascension, on your way to not only your true Self, but also to your true home."

24

The Missing Piece

I wondered how much understanding of his discoveries Christopher would retain. From my own experience, I realize how new insights must be repeated many times before the psyche can incorporate them. The disconnected psyche becomes powerful in its repetitive patterning; old habits are not easily discarded.

Christopher and Margaret came together to his next session, two weeks later, to clarify why, despite all the work he had done to balance his male and female energies, his ambivalence toward her persisted. He was eager to explain what had occurred since the last session. He was in a heightened consciousness, and neither of us wished to interrupt him:

> *I returned home with good intentions.*
> *Margaret looked at me and was delighted.*
> *I responded to her from my new male self*
> *and embraced her tenderly with the energy*
> *of my female. She had been waiting for this*
> *transformation.*
>
> *We connected as one being.*
> *We felt our love for one another,*

*but when our physical consummation ended,
I was thrown again into an ambivalent state.*

*I could not sustain my contact with her.
It had disappeared.
I fought to regain it.
I felt betrayed.
What abyss had I fallen into?*

*Courageously I entered the abyss.
I saw my body spinning in the mist.
I shouted incoherently to someone
from an inner depth.
I screamed: I can't, I won't,
I won't recognize You, God.*

*I screamed out to You for centuries.
You never answered.
I stopped screaming
and became mad as hell.
My rage I refuse to give You.*

*I'll live without You.
No ups, no downs.
Just a monotonous boredom.
I won't give You my wrath.
You cast me down
to be an ordinary mortal.*

*I thought I was special,
an angel by Your side.
Why this separation from You?
Have I deserved the brutal lives*

> *I've lived?*
> *Did You ordain them?*
> *Enough of Your punishment.*
>
> *I no longer blame my earthly parents.*
> *Why do I still blame You?*
> *Is blaming You the reason*
> *I can't find my angelic Self?*

Christopher opened his eyes and looked as if from a great distance at Margaret and me. "I'm stuck," he moaned.

I suggested that he ask God to help him become unstuck. He hesitated, but with a little encouragement continued.

> *My separation from You keeps me drifting.*

There was another silence, then he went on again.

> *Enlighten me with Your wisdom.*
> *I am ready to hear the truth.*

And the answer came:

> **Christopher, you were and still are of**
> **my substance.**
> **As a newborn soul, you wanted more.**
> **But the more had to be tempered**
> **and transmuted.**
>
> **In the heavenly sphere,**
> **learning is the reason to exist.**
> **Learning gives the soul its dimension.**

You refused this undertaking.
You separated from Me
and fell into despair.

You've lived in deep despair in
this life, and
in many others as well.
Know
when you connect to your intrinsic
Self,
your separation from me
will end.

Your separation from me
comes from your willfulness.
Connect with Me and it will
be mended.

Give me your rage.
Rage is healthier than withdrawal.
Shout your pain of separation
from Me
from the rafters.
I will smile at your acknowledgment.
Your wrath toward your parents has
been clarified.
Now do the same toward Me.

Shout, Christopher!
Shout!
Shout with an open heart!

Christopher had tears in his eyes at this point.

> *God, God, or whatever*
> *You are called.*
> *I want to return to You.*
> *I have been angry, furious.*
> *I cast You away.*
> *I am ready to return.*
>
> *I come to You with longing;*
> *trepidation, too.*
> *Will You accept me as I am?*
> *Open Your arms.*
> *I'm ready for Your embrace.*

Christopher paused briefly as the inner Voice continued:

> **Your shouts warm my heart.**
> **They resound throughout**
> **the universe.**
> **I have regained an angel for my**
> **realm.**
> **Shout, Christopher!**
> **Shout!**
> **Shout your want of Me.**

Christopher answered softly:

> *God!*
> *I am part of You.*
> *I am.*

Margaret and I were silent. Christopher's face shone. He turned to her and spoke gently. "What has just happened is real for me. I asked you to come to the session because I knew there was a more profound explanation for my vacillation. And you know how sick I am of this stupid vacillation. You're also sick of it. But I have unfinished business with God and until I connect solidly to the Essence, I'll be restless and unpredictable with my feelings toward you. It's not fair to you. I ask you to give me more time, time in which I can solidify my higher-self relationship."

Margaret scrutinized him carefully and said, "I understand what you're saying. The difference in you is astounding. I'll wait, but not too long. I also know that you are incredibly self-indulgent."

25

Fulfillment

Christopher and Margaret were scheduled for a six-month dance tour overseas. This event brought our therapeutic work to a halt for the immediate future. They were excited about their new adventure, which would culminate in a three-week vacation in Bali. Since Bali is an exotic, romantic country, Christopher hoped he would be ready for a marital decision and a Balinese wedding.

Christopher:

Our trip is a great success. Margaret and I are sharing our lives in ways that are wonderful. We feel closer to one another than ever; but within me is always the gnawing feeling that I don't want to commit myself to her. I don't show her my agony, but I'm sure she senses it. How I long to speak further with you, but perhaps my absence from the sessions will force me to think more deeply about my dilemma by myself.

I sit daily in the Buddhist temples while Margaret is shopping in the markets. I sit as though transfixed by the serene, elevated atmosphere the monks create as they meditate. I find myself leaving the earth and going to worlds beyond the earth. There, my psyche and my soul search for the way to the Essence. The search for and the yearning for God, if you want to call it that, is so intense within me that I am ecstatically filled with purpose.

I crash when I have to engage in mundane talk about the articles Margaret purchased. I crash when she wants physical contact. I crash when she brings up the idea of marriage. I crash when her need for contact becomes dominant and we bicker about how to spend our time together. I love her but I'm still ambivalent about marrying her.

I want at this time of my life to explore my connection to God. Is this self-indulgence? Is it another ploy to avoid commitment to a woman? I'm sure there are elements of my usual avoidance in the matter, but I can't deny that when I am alone and involved in this search, I feel joy. This joy is greater than sharing my life with Margaret or any other woman. This joy feels like a necessity I can no longer deny myself.

Do I need to probe more to get a clearer balance between the male and female energies? The answer is, "Yes!" But at present, my more unified male and female energies are directing me toward God. If I suppress this momentum, I'm afraid I'll be repeating an ancient pattern of denial.

When I ask my soul for answers, it says: "Follow your heart."

My response:

You have dealt with the male and female issues in your psyche. You have a woman who loves you and whom you love. With regard to further commitment, however, it is as though your psyche pulls down a metal shutter, such as store owners pull down over their stores' glass windows at the end of their workday. You are behind the shutters, alone, not knowing where to go, what to do next. Christopher, you do know what to do next, but you cannot quite accept what you know.

Perhaps there is another way to understand your dilemma. Might not your constant falling back into ambivalence be the result of your soul's voice telling you that at present you have more urgent business to attend to than your relationship with a woman? The urgent business is your reacquaintance with your divinity. Your soul is closing the metal shutters from further connection with Margaret because your connection to God is still too fragile to combine it with an earthly love relationship. You might too easily slip into negative patterns, bringing forth more denial of

God. If this is truly the case, recognize it and let go of Margaret so that she can move into her life without you.

Manifest your urgent, unfinished divine business by looking for satisfying ways of fulfilling your quest instead of perpetually being at odds with it.

Christopher dedicated himself to evolving, searching for his Godself. He and Margaret separated. She continued with her own personal growth. They parted as friends but did not keep in touch.

Three years passed. Accidentally one day, Margaret and Christopher met. He said:

> *I'm ready,*
> *ready for you,*
> *my true love.*
> *I'm ready for God,*
> *my first love.*
> *My soul*
> *will never vacillate*
> *again,*
> *because we three*
> *are one.*

They married, live happily together, and continue even today to work on themselves.

Part Three

Didi

26

The Soul of Didi

I'm back again.
Get out of my way.
It was a devastating experience
down there.

Where's my compartment?
I want it as I left it.
Angel of Destiny:
"Appear!"

It's always so quiet.
They're all filled with fear.
Well, this time
I'll go when I'm ready.

Do You hear me, God,
angel, Council?
I'll go when I'm ready.
Not before.

Everyone knows I'm special.
They got the message down there.
I'm God's personal helper,
His right-hand angel.
How did He fare in my
absence?

He hasn't been told
I'm back.
That's okay.
He'll rush to see me
when He hears.

I'll rest in the meantime.
I'll put up a sign,
NOT TO BE DISTURBED
UNTIL I SAY SO.

That does it.
Now for a siesta,
a sweet, long repose.
I'll be refreshed for
my meeting with God.
We'll speak about Earth
matters.
He'll wish to have
first-hand information.

I dream about God and me.
It was sweet at first.
But in my dream,
suddenly I was cast
out of the firmament.

*I grasped its sides
with my fingertips,
screaming,
"God, it's not time!
I've just returned.
You wouldn't do this
to Your favorite angel.
You'd ask my consent
about my going back so
soon.*

*"Wouldn't you do that
for me?"*

*I awaken,
I shake myself vehemently.
My compartment is dark.
Could the Angel of Destiny
be casting his shadow before
my habitat?*

*God!
Have You forsaken me?*

*I race past the angel,
almost crushing his wings.
I enter the Council chambers.
I scream,
"By whose decree
do you send me down?"
"By God's, of course,"
they reply.*

*"I'll not go down
until I see God personally."
The sages are dumbfounded.*

*"Soul, lovely soul,
accept God's decision.
Rectify your delusion
of coequal status.
You are you,
not God."*

*I weep bitterly,
convinced God has betrayed me.
I go with the Angel of Destiny.
The sages look on,
sending me loving energy,
"Call on us when you need
our help."*

*I sit opposite the angel
in the silvery net.
He tries to make me feel
better.
I am stubborn and prideful;
I'll have none of it.*

*As we land on Earth,
I feel remorse.
I smile at him as
he makes a last effort
to give me compassion
and heartfelt love.*

*The male and female
are copulating.
She wants a child.
The angel puts me
into her womb.
"It's a passionate act,"
I think, "but the
woman abhors it."*

*The male wishes to mount
her again.
She tells him emphatically,
"Not without my permission!"*

*"Oh, God!" I call to the Elders.
"There will be no love here.
Give me the courage to go
through this life.
It's going to be difficult."*

*The Elders immerse me in
their warm support.
I accept it and am grateful.
I keep thinking of the beauty
of the universe,
to sustain my nine-month
incarceration.*

*I keep in mind that the earth
is a schoolhouse,
helping me cleanse and purify.
I also remember the ultimate
goal:
to return home,
home to God's world.*

27

The First Session with Didi

I sat in my office, enjoying the precious ten-minute break between sessions. The waiting room had a telephone mounted on a wall. My reprieve was broken by raucous shrieking. When I opened my office door, I saw my new patient on the telephone, pounding the instrument like a boxer pounding an opponent. She was engaged in a loud, fierce argument with someone called Rita.

When she saw me, her eyes widened. She slammed the receiver onto the metal hook with such ferocity that paint chipped off the telephone, scattering on the floor. I looked at the damaged receiver, picked the paint chips off the floor, and threw them into the wastepaper basket. The new patient stared at me, then grabbed her belongings and ran into my office, smiling broadly, with the energy of which storms are made.

I shook her hand and asked her to sit in a chair opposite mine. She sat far back in the chair, then wiggled forward to the edge of it, leaning as far toward me as she could.

When she was settled in a position acceptable to her, she volunteered: "That was Rita, my mom. What a pest! I can't do anything right in her eyes. If she'd been near me, she would have slapped me in the face or on my back, even now, when I'm twenty-five. What a mockery, what a lie— honor your father and mother! If I had honored her, I'd be dead! I liked reading Alice Miller's book about abusive parents. She, too, thought honoring abusive parents was a mockery. What do you think? By the way, I'm Didi."

"Welcome, Didi. I gather that you and your mother are not well-disposed toward one another."

"Not well-disposed? That's an understatement. I loathe her! I can say that with conviction and without guilt, because I've already had six years of Bioenergetic therapy. I used to express my anger toward her by beating the bed so ferociously with the tennis racquet that one day, the racquet broke. My former therapist was a man. He and I laughed so hard and long that my belly hurt for days.

"Rita's been that way as far back as I can remember. She has a violent temper and smacked me around all the time. I'd talk back to her, which would infuriate her more; but I couldn't stop myself. I guess it was the only way I could maintain any self-esteem. I was a skinny kid. Food would go through me. They said I must have a tapeworm, but I didn't. I think my system got caught up in avoiding her wrath and outsmarting her so she would lay off me. That effort must have burned up all the food I ate."

I watched Didi's body language throughout her long but vibrant and interesting explanation. Now she changed her position at the edge of her chair, apparently because she felt she had my full attention. Like a yogi, she assumed a half-lotus position, crossing one leg over the other thigh. I remarked to myself how flexible she was. I asked her if she was involved with yoga training. She said she wasn't, looked at the position of her legs and told me she was just comfortable in this position. She was ready to continue with her explanation when, out of curiosity, I asked: "You say you've been in Bioenergetic analysis for six years? Why are you here?"

"Well, I'm here because my therapist, Dr. Brandon, died six months ago, on the heels of my father's death of pancreatic cancer. Dr. Brandon died of heart failure. He helped me with my father's death. That was important, because I was left in the house with Rita and, as you already know, dealing with her is no joke. So, now I'm an orphan. I don't have a natural father or a substitute 'good daddy' any more."

Suddenly Didi unwound herself from her leg position and sat back in her chair. She no longer had any awareness of me but was involved in the loss of her deceased therapist who, she said, had "seen her through her early wilderness." Tears filled her eyes as she recalled his goodness to her. Her body relaxed. She no longer felt the need to be engaging. I saw a forlorn, lost person in front of me. I learned that at nineteen she had her first session with Dr. Brandon after having smoked hashish. She had split off from herself so badly that she had felt totally lost. She felt he had mended her split without medication: with care, with insight, with Bioenergetic work. She repeated again what a terrible loss his death was, not only to herself but to others who were helped by him.

She sobbed deeply. Her body was convulsed with her pain. As I gave her tissues, she grabbed my hands and pleaded, "Will you fill the void? Will you guide me and support me? I'm a hard worker, not a shirker. I need to fill the emptiness until I can find myself. I don't want to do it with drugs. Somehow I've always known that drugs were not the solution, even when I was surrounded by friends who thought they were. Most of them still don't know and they're freaked out, miserable, and lost. I have to help myself first before I can help them. Don't you agree?"

She held my hands more tightly. With deep sincerity she said: "I feel your energy and I like it. I want to work with you."

"I feel a great deal of compassion for your situation," I said. "You've done excellent work with Dr. Brandon. I'd be delighted to help you. Your honesty, directness, and desire to grow are refreshing."

Didi quickly wiped her eyes. "Okay, okay. Let's start."

Before I could respond, she took off her clothes, stripping down to her brassiere and underwear. She assumed I wanted to diagnose her body.

I laughed heartily. "Okay, Didi, let's start. Get in front of the mirror. Let's look at your body and begin our work together."

I saw a thin, emaciated body. I inwardly agreed with Didi that she had used all of her energy to fight off her violent mother. The most startling armoring, however, was her pelvis. Not in alignment with the rest of her body, it was drastically pulled back, as if to ward off another's invasive sexual energy.

I asked her about her sexual feelings. She described herself as "hot," but said she attracted mostly passive men. She assumed that macho men were not interested in her, because she was not a beauty like her mother. "I'm orgasmic, but I don't let go completely. I'm aware that I hold back, but I never unraveled this issue with my former therapist. I'll do it with you. It might be easier because you're a woman."

I noted her comments, then concentrated on her contracted chest and armored upper back. I asked her how this region of her body felt. She said, "It feels as though Mom is on my back. When I was a kid, I discovered that when I contracted my back muscles tightly, I would feel the blows from her fists less. But in warding off her blows to my back, I contracted my chest so much that now I can't stretch out my arms; they've foreshortened. They became too immobilized either to push her off or to reach out to anyone for help.

"But earlier than her fist blows, I know for a fact that she didn't breast-feed me or hold me. She let me lie alone in my crib, sucking my fingers until they got puckery. I'll be damned if I'll continue to let myself be stuck in these abuses forever."

I was delighted by her determination. "Good for you, Didi! In the meantime, you have daddy in your pelvis and mom in your upper back and chest. When I look at your feet and legs and your lack of grounding, I sense you want to fly away, out of this life."

"I sure have trouble being here," Didi agreed. "When I was little, I was always away from our household in friends' homes. I would silently adopt everyone else's parents as mine. Everyone's mom was better than Rita. Gary, my father, was seldom home. He worked crazy hours in the garment district, so I didn't see much of him. I do remember that the rare times when he was at home and he put me on his lap, I would jump off like a fly off a hot griddle."

I asked her if this observation meant anything to her. She thought about my question for a long time. "I guess I couldn't trust him either," she finally said, sadly.

She then changed to another topic. "I was born in Brooklyn, New York, of a Jewish background—but no one ever explained to either my brother Randy or me what it meant to be Jewish. He's four years older and my mom's favorite. She never hit him, although she wanted to. He must have given her a strong message to lay off. I wish I knew Randy's secret. Talk about armoring. You should see his body. I don't know of anyone who could crack such a shell. He worked with my therapist for a while, too, but when he died, Randy was so upset he said he would never be vulnerable to anyone again. By now he doesn't know whether he's going or coming. Even so I put him on a pedestal. He's a good friend and will always come through when I need him. That's comforting, but I sometimes feel we're two blind people trying to help each other see."

She hesitated, becoming aware of how quickly she was speaking and explaining. "I'm jumping all over the place. I want you to know everything in one session."

"I understand the feeling, Didi," I said. "As though you want to compress your entire life and six therapeutic years into one hour."

"I just want to move ahead and not waste time. It seems I made a pact with myself in some forgotten time to clean up my act and ship out fast in this life."

"Did you ever think your urgency might come from a desire to resolve ancient difficulties, and to do it as quickly as possible so you can feel the truth of your soul?"

Didi's eyes shone. "You know that feeling too, don't you? I knew I'd come to the right place." She stood quickly, realizing the time was up. "I'll see you next week."

As she passed through the waiting room she looked at the telephone receiver she had mutilated. "I'll bring you a new phone next week, same color. I made a mess."

28

Didi's Father and the Men in Her Life

In the next session, Didi again placed herself in the chair opposite mine and assumed the same forward position with her body. I had the disturbing impression that I could be eaten alive by the neediness hidden behind her garrulous and accessible manner. However, I also felt the strong current of her life force and the dramatic fullness of her nature. She was ready to go on with her story.

I made myself ready, drawn in by her extraordinary energy, her desire to disentangle her complicated psyche and to discover her true Self.

"Well, here I am," she said. "I couldn't wait to come again. My friends say I'm always shooting off my mouth. I guess they mean I do a lot of self-searching, feel a lot of things. But I need someone to help me sort out the information that comes to the surface. I brought pictures of my parents. I know you didn't ask for them, but I thought it would speed things up." She smiled at me mischievously as she added: "You know I've got a better place to go to when I'm through here on this Earth, so I want to make sure I'm as squeaky clean psychically as I can be."

Without warning Didi stood up and did a tap routine, singing: "Open up those pearly gates, I'm coming through. I've been away a long, long time, too long away from You." She ended the song she had spontaneously created by pointing to the sky, then looked at me for my approval.

I laughed heartily and praised her creativity. Then I questioned her about her dance training. From the pile of photographs she had brought, she pulled a picture of herself at the age of five in a dance costume. She explained that dance training was one of the better things her parents had provided for both Randy and her. They took tap dancing lessons as well as ballet. She said she loved this training, but after a few years and without explanation, the lessons were stopped for her, but not for her brother. She remained furious about this loss and added this resentment to the welter of other resentments that fueled her rebelliousness.

She again turned to the photographs. In total absorption, she shuffled through them until she arrived at a picture of herself facing her father. She showed it to me. I saw a tall, striking, robust, red-haired man, looking at his fourteen-year old daughter lasciviously. I reacted with shock at his undisguised sexual interest in his daughter.

Didi smiled at my reaction as an affirmation of her own feelings. She told me that even though she was very thin, she had become full-breasted at an early age and her father focused on her breasts. "That's what I grew up with," she said. "My father looked at me like a slobbering animal. He did it as well with other women—in front of my mother, his kids, all of us. His male friends did the same. It was their effort at being macho, I suppose, but to me they looked like ghouls."

Didi's rage at her father's invasion flared up. She held the photograph before her and screamed her indignation. "You nincompoop, sexual pervert. Look at how I had to fend you off with my pelvis, even from a young age, when I felt it too dangerous to even sit in your lap. Look at my pelvis now and how distorted it became as I tried to protect myself from you. I had to hide my breasts because your fiery eyes were focused on them; not on me, your daughter—but on my boobs, which you always wanted to touch. Here, little boy, here are mommy's tits. Suck them. You never got your sucking from your mother, you can't get it from Rita, so you want to suck your daughter's. What insanity."

She threw the photograph on the floor and was about to destroy it when I asked her if destroying it was what she truly wanted.

She said, "You're right! Why bother?"

I suggested that she go over the breathing stool instead and work on softening the pelvic block so, in time, the pelvis would become unified with the rest of her body.

"Then I'll no longer have him in me or live from a cockeyed sexuality." She got very excited as her insights emerged. "Then I'll no longer choose the wrong men and feel that a relationship with a man is a waste of time."

"Exactly!" Then I asked, "Did your father ever protect you from your mother's violence?"

Didi became sad. "Of course not. All he said was to stop answering her back and to stay away from her. That's what he did. As I got older, he came home later and later. I was left to fend for myself with this maniac. I used to come home from school at lunchtime because she insisted on it. I dreaded this lunchtime saga.

"One day she met me at the door and began to box me with her fists until she had me cornered in a narrow bathroom. When she was about to bang my head into the wall, I screamed so loud, the next-door neighbor ran into our apartment and pulled her away from me. I'm convinced that if the neighbor hadn't interfered, she would have killed me. To this day I don't understand what prompted that amount of violence. But thereafter, I stayed in friends' homes even longer than usual. My father and I resorted to the same way of avoiding her."

"I'm astonished you survived as well as you did," I offered, feeling I needed to let her know of her courage to stay alive.

"I suppose you're right, but when you go through such hell . . . well, I just held on to survival with my fingernails, hoping I wouldn't let go. But it feels good to get someone else's reactions to my home life."

"Did he help you, Didi?" I asked again.

"No, I didn't get help from him. He was reputed to be a violent man. I was always warned not to get him angry. I don't get it! If he was such a violent man, why was he so passive with her? He was a staunch family man with two kids. He gave her everything she wanted, even though nothing satisfied her. He worked hard. They fought bitterly with each other while Randy and I listened to her accusations that we were the cause of her misery. He flirted all the time with other women, which gave me the impression he liked women. Yet he was miserable with her, but didn't leave. I don't get it!"

"Despite your father's macho attitude, he might have been a passive man, sexually ineffectual, which could have caused your mother's extreme frustration. It's no doubt true that she was difficult to please, but my suspicion is that he brought his passivity into the relationship from his own parenting. If he came from a matriarchal background, he must have had ambivalent feelings toward his mother and women in general. Claiming sexual prowess in the blatant ways you've described indicates that he was not connected to his genitality in a healthy way. You, unfortunately, as well as your mother, became the objects of his distorted sexuality."

"You've got it right," said Didi. "He came from a matriarchal family—my grandmother ruled like a tyrant. He was her favorite. Even though my father was supposed to have beaten up a Nazi Bund leader in the subway in the forties because the guy made an anti-Jewish remark, he certainly never displayed any of this rage to defend Randy and me. Does that make sense? My mother, probably like his mother, rode over him like a Mack truck and he didn't flinch. He just avoided. What a puzzle! What a mess I've got to sort out so I can get liberated."

I asked her how her father's image affected the choice of men in her life. "I was married at twenty to an Israeli, who emigrated with me to the United States. He, too, was a macho, with even less morality than my father. When I brought my Israeli husband into one of my sessions with Dr. Brandon, the doctor remarked that my husband looked like one of the family. He was similar in appearance to my father, but even sleazier.

"Unbeknownst to me, he was a womanizer and a drug dealer. When he lifted his hands to hit me one night, when I confronted him about where he'd been, I became my mother. I hit him so hard with my fists, he backed into a corner. You can imagine the scene. This macho, who had formerly been a pilot in the Israeli air force, was reduced to a defensive little boy, attacked by a skinny runt like me. But a runt on fire! I've been asking myself since I divorced him why I chose someone even more disordered than my father. Do you have an answer?"

"You're raising an important question, Didi, but one we'll involve ourselves with later in the therapy. I believe the question can be answered from the viewpoint of Reflectivism. I use it extensively in my work, but only after a grounded therapeutic process has been established. In the meantime, tell me more: are you involved in another relationship?"

"I recently started another one, but I feel it's on the other end of the spectrum. I don't seem to find a middle ground for myself. What I'm saying is that as much as my husband was macho and distorted, Alan is passive: sweet but undefined. He's an antidote to my father and my ex-husband, but I'm afraid I feel bored a good part of the time."

"Why bored?"

"I don't know why. I'm not sure. So I blame myself, thinking I've been used to living in a violent, unloving, mucked-up atmosphere and that anything that doesn't have the high-wire tension of my home life is less exciting. I must think a more quiet environment bores me. I don't know. I'm just feeling it through. With your help, I hope to get an answer.

"But a valid reason for boredom is that the sex is so-so. He fades away fast—that is, he loses his erection quickly. But I get tenderness from him, which is a rare experience in my life with men. He's a cook, and it's wonderful to be served delicious meals every night after a harrowing day in the garment district. I guess I'll soak up some of the softness and sweetness he's capable of. When I feel bored and want to fight it, I can't get enough of those qualities. We also have three cats."

"You've surrounded yourself with the feline nature," I chuckled. "Drink it in, Didi, and let's see how so much tenderness and sweetness will register in your psyche."

"Okay, I'll drink it in. It's better than being disappointed and scared all the time."

As Didi left, she told me that I would find a surprise in the waiting room. She then dashed away, grinning from ear to ear.

Upon opening the waiting room door, I saw a new, bright, green phone hanging on the wall. I laughed with delight at the brilliant color, at Didi's unpredictable nature, and at her generosity.

29

Didi's Mother

"How can I speak about Rita without wanting to put her against a wall and pummel her to a slow, painful death?" began Didi in her next session. "I feel bad about having so much hatred toward another human being, but I can't think of a single redeeming quality in that woman. I recall when I was about four years old, I used to play with her dimpled, fat elbow, put my mouth to it, and suck as though it were a breast. At first she would laugh uproariously, but soon would push me away harshly. It was the only physical closeness with her I remember, and for that reason I'd like to pulverize her.

"My brother Randy was the firstborn. Of course, in a Jewish family he was considered a prince of the blood. I was less important because I was a girl and came along four years later. This made the household complete and perfect according to the cultural values of the time. No one thought about the fact that it had taken Rita eight years to conceive Randy. No one knew that after that eight years of trying to get pregnant, my parents were in the process of adopting a child. Finally, the willful Rita submitted to Gary's sperm. Her narcissism had blocked her from getting pregnant until it dawned on her he would be less committed, less slavelike without the bond of a baby. When she produced two children, a boy and a girl, her fate was secure. Rita and Gary were hailed the perfect couple.

"What a farce! But was she honest enough to think of it that way? Naah! She just kept on going, as though she were the epitome of perfection. Her adoring father treated her like she was royalty and gave her more than her two older sisters. She was smothered in fur coats at an early age and given singing and dance lessons. She got everything she wanted, and boy, she wanted everything. She primed herself for a theatrical career, but when she wanted to work in the theater, her father put his foot down with a vengeance."

"What form did that take?" I asked.

"This will shock you, but he literally pulled her off the stage when she was rehearsing in a show and forbade her to ever return to the theater."

"How did your mother react to that kind of forceful behavior?"

"I think she was bewildered by it, and confused. Their connection to each other was so screwy, she couldn't see straight."

"By screwy, you mean there was an incestuous quality to it?"

"I guess so. She couldn't say no to him, even though she was devastated by his behavior. But nothing stopped her. She was going to get what she wanted from the man no matter what. So she married Gary, a man her father detested. No man was good enough for his beloved, indulged daughter. You know I think you're right about incest. Her father had such a secret passion for her, he never would have let go of her if Rita hadn't married my father. She quickly cast him into the Gary-daddy role and proceeded to bleed him dry just like her father."

"This sounds like the height of narcissism."

"You think that's narcissism? Listen to this. She told us about an incident that happened with her sisters when she was twelve. Her sisters were fed up with her insatiable demands and mean spirit, so one day they took a large pillow and covered Rita's head, intending to smother and kill her."

At the mention of her mother being killed, Didi's body doubled over with laughter.

"You would like to have done the same?"

"Would I ever!" said Didi. "But no such luck. Anyway, her father heard her muffled screams, came into the room, and rescued her. She was nearly unconscious. But listen to the rest of it! My mother tells the story, *proud* of her *favoritism* with her father and proud of her powerful role in the family! *Bitch, Rita! You're an unprecedented, stupid bitch!*"

Didi continued: "How did she get away with so much selfishness all her life? I can't get away with anything."

I looked at her intently. "Do you really want to get away with selfishness or other irresponsible behavior?"

She shook her head.

"You shake your head, but I'm not convinced," I said. "Let me remind you that we earn our right to ascension in the most minute, seemingly insignificant ways. If you're unsure about the right or wrong path, you'll be tested—which is the fate for all of us.

"This might be the right time to introduce the concept of Reflectivism. Remember that Rita is your mother in this life because you chose her prenatally, and with your having chosen such a woman, you will have to consider that you are a mirror reflection of her. So don't feel sorry for yourself about not getting away with misdeeds. Be glad, because unlike her, you'll not build up the amount of karma she accumulated due to her unconsciousness."

Didi listened pensively. "I'm ready for more, but I don't know if this kind of 'more' is what I can look at right now. It's difficult to accept that I'm a reflection of such a hateful woman. Right now I'm more involved with Alan's sexual impotence. I feel as though I want to nullify everything about him because of his limp penis. Is this the Rita in me or am I justified in wanting to castrate him?"

"Alan has a sexual problem," I agreed. "He is a passive man, which indicates that his mother usurped his sexual energy. Wasn't this also the case with Gary, your father? Since Gary served as a role model for the impressionable little Didi, isn't it logical that you would gravitate toward men who are passive? Your husband was more potent, but he needed other women to bolster his male ego. Don't you see? You choose men who represent missing aspects in your own nature. Your male and female energies are not balanced. If this imbalance is not addressed, you'll rave and rant at the injustices of Rita and Gary until you die.

"Didi, you can do it. You have a good understanding of your parents and their effect on your psyche. But if you keep blaming them, you will become a martyr and wallow in your martyrdom forever. Let's move on. You are readier than you think you are."

"Do you mean I like the stuck place I'm at?" Didi asked thoughtfully. "I have to admit that feeling like a victim does keep me wallowing in deprivation. I don't have to look at myself except as the abused one."

"That's right, Didi. It's a place that becomes very comfortable and gets you a lot of attention—for a little while. Others' attitudes toward you will be: 'Poor little Didi, her life was hard. We mustn't ask too much of her. Poor little waif.' Finally, though, they will catch on or get weary of being supportive."

"That sounds pathetic, but I think you're right. What will I find out about myself if I look further? A lot of ugly stuff! Won't that make me feel more horrible than I already do?"

"Yes, but the door to your real self will stay open, not shut as it will be if you don't take the next step."

She was pensive. "I know if I don't face it, I'll never get to the real me, the best and most complete part of me—my Godself."

"That's right. And what's more important, Didi, is that unless you face what you perceive as the ugly stuff within you, you will not find the real, the good stuff either. 'Ugly stuff' is unconscious stuff; but it's also what will help you learn about yourself and give you the motivation and energy to change.

"You'll reach a point where you need so desperately to find the real You that you are willing to turn your old self inside out. Shaking out the old stuff will allow the true female and male energies to become available. And, guess what? They will connect you to your Godself. Isn't that what you've been wanting ever since you came to me?"

She nodded. "I guess I'll have to bite the bullet," she said. "But, let's wait until the next session."

30

Didi's Female and Male Energies

In her next session, Didi was quieter than usual. She told me she had never felt so frightened as at that moment. She said that if she actually reflected her mother, she had fooled herself all her life by believing she was successfully fighting not to be like her.

Most patients who have hateful parents do make deliberate, concentrated efforts not to resemble them. However, as much as a person fights to be unlike the hated parents, the parents' energies, lodged in the psyche of the patient, will emerge at unexpected and unguarded times.

"Didi, you tell me you want to destroy Alan for his sexual impotence. Do you have a similar urge to destroy a disabled person? No? Consider this: Alan, in his sexual impotence, is disabled. Your overreaction to the situation is what deserves your attention, because it is not only the quality of your mother, but it's also your own quality when you don't get what you want."

"But I talk to him and tell him we can work on the problem together," she answered. "As a matter of fact, we'll come to the next session together so you can meet him. Maybe he'll be interested in doing some work on this issue."

"The fact remains, Didi, that you still want to destroy him. So let's look into all of this. Let's start with your left side, your female side, to see if your body experience will clarify what I'm trying to explain. Stretch your left arm, starting with the left hand, until your body moves into another position. Connect with the feelings as well as the movement."

As Didi knew, the exercise I suggested was based on the principle that every human being contains a duality of being—one of male energies and female energies—and that each of these energies is expressed in one of the halves of the body. The right half is regarded as expressing the male energy; the left, the female energy. I have found that this principle is reflective of truth and is of the greatest value in helping others understand and accept the deepest motivations in their behavior.

Didi got to her feet sullenly. Because she was a kinetic, emotional being, however, getting caught up in the exercise didn't take her long. She stretched her left side and, as she did so, the fingers of her left hand began alternately to curl and uncurl. With that curling, she began to grimace. She was obeying her impulses and moving emotionally from them.

She focused on an image that was before her. She scratched at the thing as though she were eviscerating it, screaming out with pleasure: "I want to tear your flesh. I want to tear your body apart. I want to tear off your penis and throw it away for not giving me pleasure. You owe me. I want, I want! Give it all to me so I'm satisfied! Nothing satisfies me! God doesn't satisfy me! Nothing is enough!"

As I looked at the ravenous beastlike character before me, I saw Rita's nature replicated. Didi looked grotesque. She stomped around the room with her claws extended, ripping at everything she touched. She raged until her energy was spent. Then she lowered her arm, and as she slowly came back to reality, I saw that the look in her eyes was one of fury and an intent to kill.

I held her left hand, bringing warmth to her left side. Didi's eyes returned slowly to their normal, bright look as she recognized me. She shook her head, as if to toss off the imagery she had been involved in, at the same time grabbing my hands to make certain that support for her experience was really there. When she was reassured, she spoke.

"That's Rita, isn't it? Is it really me, too? I sometimes go into these rages and I want a lot, a hell of a lot. I've managed to control that temperament, though, because I don't want to be like Rita. This energy is in my psyche, nevertheless. I've been pushing it down. I camouflage it with a lot of understanding, becoming an oracle for others. They seek me out and I give good advice, but while I'm doing it, I'm always involved in thinking I'm hot stuff. That way I hide from the fact that I really want to clobber them for making demands on me."

Didi remained quiet for a long time while she thought about her experience of her female side. She asked me why her left side was so unfeminine.

"Is your mother's energy feminine, Didi? When you reflect your mother's energy, are you feminine?"

"No, a thousand times no!" she exclaimed. "It's bestial in her and in me, too, when I allow that energy to come through."

"I'm certain that your mother's female energy is male-dominated because she ingested her father's domineering male energy and couldn't relate to her mother's weak, almost nonexistent female energy. Sometimes male and female energies replace each another. They switch roles. It's one form of gender imbalance. Rita's unwillingness to connect to her mother's energy left her without a female self."

I noticed that Didi's attention was wandering. "Are you following me?"

"I think so. You're saying that even though Rita lives in a female body, she's so much identified with her father that his aggressive, self-involved, violent male energy became her overriding way of being."

"Right on, Didi. It makes her devoid of feminine softness, receptivity, or creativity."

"Which means that I, like her, have replaced my female energy with my father's passive, macho, self-indulgent qualities."

"Correct. But remember: once you realize this, you can search for the true, God-given selves that are inside you." I paused, letting her digest what had been said. "It's appropriate right now to explore your male energy, to look into why your unconscious, like Rita's, resorted to switching the male and female energies."

I saw a blank look on her face. "Can you handle more? If not, we'll slow things down."

"I'm overwhelmed, that's all," said Didi, on the verge of tears. "But deep inside, I feel your explanation makes sense." She then justified being overwhelmed, telling me, "Since I'm mostly an experiential person, I'll wait to work with my male side to decide if your theory is right."

I noted to myself that I'd seen a bit of arrogance in her.

"The psyche is complicated, isn't it?" she added, realizing inwardly she had become resistant and that her immediate response was one of knowing better than me.

I ignored her reaction, desiring foremost that she understand. "Yes, the psyche is extremely complicated, especially when you consider the complexities of the parents' behavior, the psyche's sensitivity to that behavior, and the larger karmic endowment each of us must struggle with."

She shrugged. "I have no choice but to look at my male side. Let's start."

"Good for you, Didi! Begin by stretching your right side, just as you did with the left side, the female side."

I watched as she experimented with stretching her male side. After the first movement impulse, she spontaneously took several small, falling steps forward, with her right arm and hand reaching toward something or someone. She repeated the forward, falling leg motion, continuing to reach with her right arm.

I instructed her to voice what she was feeling. She did so in small frightened tones.

"Mamma, Mamma, where are you? Don't leave me alone. I need you. Come here!" Repeating these phrases brought forth the despair behind her words. Those despairing feelings pulled Didi to the floor, where she sobbed plaintively. Crouched on her hands and knees, she beat the floor with her right hand, screaming, "Don't leave me alone. Look at me. Don't turn away. I don't want to be left alone!"

Eventually her sobbing subsided. She slowly returned to a sitting position on the floor. Rubbing her eyes with her hands when she had regained her composure, she said sadly: "If this is my male side, it's pretty pathetic. These feelings should be coming from the female side. Not that males don't cry, but I never realized there was so much despair in me. It makes me wonder if I've ever related to anyone from my female side."

"Good for you, Didi. You can now understand how you've juxtaposed your female energy onto the male energy. Do you understand how unbalanced this makes you?"

"I wonder what happens to the soft, needy feelings? I guess I cover them up with bravado, like Gary, my father. The bravado says, 'I don't need anyone. I'm macho.' It says, 'Come here, babe, let me touch your tits.'" Didi was silent, searching, trying to understand more about this mysterious place in her psyche. Suddenly she burst forth: "That's it! That's the basis of his breast fetish. He's always reaching for the breast his mother never gave him. I'm involved in the same pattern. I've never let myself know how severe the deprivation was. Instead, I've covered it up with my mother's obnoxious arrogance and my father's arrogant macho posturing." She mimicked her reactions: *"Me, needy? Me? You must be crazy! Does anyone ever see me ask for help? Never!"*

"That's right," I said. "Your unwillingness to feel the depth of your despair and your neediness makes you hang on more tenaciously to the arrogance. It's a vicious circle, and the longer you stay in it, the harder you will have to fight to get out of it."

"I'm dazed. I've got a lot to think about. I hope I can retain it."

And she looked dazed—but alive.

"Don't forget. Alan is coming to the next session."

"Fine," I said. "And here's a powerful hug from my male side."

I held her strongly, so much so that she lost her breath for a moment. She chuckled with pleasure.

I said, "I look forward to meeting him."

31

Alan

Didi and Alan sat nervously in the waiting room. The immediate impression I had when I was introduced to Alan was of him as a badgered, anxious human being. He managed a frightened smile when I shook his hand. I took them into my office and showed them where to sit. Didi felt comfortable in her usual chair, though ill-at-ease about the coming experience. She spoke up, saying she'd had a few horrible days after her last session. I was not surprised. I asked her what was so horrible about them.

"Well, I asked Alan if he was affected by my aggressive, sometimes violent, arrogant, female energy."

I turned to Alan expectantly. Instead of answering directly, he turned to Didi for permission. She gave permission, but with a slight edge of exasperation.

"It does frighten me," he responded hesitantly, "but I guess we're good together because her assertive manner makes up for my lack of aggression." He once again looked at Didi for approval.

Didi, frustrated, spoke sharply. "Alan, you're here for yourself, not to please me. So stand on your own feet and use the time effectively."

Alan pulled back, but made an effort to continue. "Well, it's been hard, because our sex life isn't working. I can't seem to please her. It wasn't that way at the beginning of our relationship, which is about two years old. I do whatever I can to please her, but what pleased her two years ago or even a few months ago doesn't work today. I'm at my wits' end and I don't know anymore what to do. That's why I came."

I saw the same look of irritation pass quickly across Didi's features. She was trying hard to keep her exasperation with him under control.

She said, "Since I became aware of my aggressive female energy in the last session, I've tried to be more gentle, more giving, less demanding. But no matter how much my attitude improves, the sex remains the same. How do you explain it, Alan? You tell me to be patient, but I've been patient. At the beginning of the relationship I was taken in by your kindness and your sweetness, but I can't tolerate any longer having to take care of myself sexually."

Alan looked away from Didi in embarrassment. "Be patient," he said. "I cook for you and take care of your other needs. This one is too much for me."

Didi flared up. "What do you mean, too much for you? It's what a man and woman do together. They have sex with an erect penis. I constantly have to stroke you to erection and then when you enter me, you become limp. What's that about? I'm frustrated and upset. My energy is too fired up anyway. Don't you think I need some sexual satisfaction from you as well as good meals? We're here to understand whether it's all my fault or whether you also have some responsibility in the matter."

Alan was distraught and humiliated. I suggested that both of them release their anger on the bed. Alan refused, saying that all had been well in their relationship until Didi became involved in the therapeutic process with me several months earlier. He claimed that since then, Didi had turned into a different person.

Didi again flared. "Now you want to blame this woman and the therapy I'm doing with her? You were this way sexually when I first met you. This has to do with you and me, not the therapist. Do you want to look at your role or not?"

Alan turned on me. "This is all your fault. She's not the same Didi I met two years ago. The Didi I love is the Didi from that time. You changed her."

I began to explain about the therapeutic process. Ignoring me, Alan left his chair, tapping Didi on the shoulder. "I'll be gone by the time you get home. I don't want any of this. It's too upsetting. I liked it when you appreciated me and weren't so demanding. I can't take your violent demands anymore."

At the door he glanced back at Didi, as though hoping she would stop him or come with him. Didi, however, just sat there stunned. Alan walked out of my office. We listened to the outer door slam behind him.

"I can't believe he's doing this. He doesn't mean it. He won't leave me." She paused. "He's never shown this much anger before, though."

Didi sat in her chair in total frustration. After a minute she went to the bed, where she released her fury at being misunderstood, at being the only one who wanted the truth, at Alan's conviction that she was the one with a "screwed-up" psyche. She was frightened by Alan's threat to leave, however. She convinced herself that he would be at home when she got there.

"Didi," I said, "Alan left this room because he was uncomfortable and unwilling to face his sexual problem. He is leaving you for the same reason. Since you were fairly content in the relationship for two years, he will use therapy and me as the cause for your dissatisfaction.

"You chose Alan as a mate because he is functioning only from female energy. After the experience with your Israeli husband, you gravitated toward a softer, more giving male. This is true of Alan. You bathed in his softness for a while, even though his sexuality was amiss. He is in a psychological position similar to yours, in that he replaced his male identity with an exaggerated female identity.

"If you weren't in search of the real Didi, you might have tolerated the imbalance between you. You might have continued functioning from your distorted Rita-like aggression. This gave his distorted male energy motivation. Conversely, you might have accepted his exaggerated female energy, substituted it for your female energy, and looked no farther.

"Many people make such contracts with one another. Many live securely, although unhappily, in such a state. Our souls know the lessons we need to take on in a given lifetime. Your soul is one that wants rectification and redemption. You need to understand that the choices you have made thus far in your life have not been happenstance. You are in an evolving state, moving gradually but definitively to ascension."

I suggested she attend my ongoing group, where she would get the support she needed for her present difficulties.

"It's obvious that I'm upset about what happened here with Alan. So your invitation comes at a good time. You're right. I'll be needing a lot of support. I still hope Alan will be home when I get there. I want to go now. There's a lot to think about."

I hugged her, but could feel her tension . . . her need to go to her apartment.

32

Didi's Introduction to the Group

At the group meeting Didi greeted those she knew and, in her extroverted way, introduced herself to those she did not know. She looked comfortable though strained. I asked her what had occurred with Alan since her last session and suggested that she tell the group members so they could help her. Didi was open to them, looking at each person as she spoke.

"It's been tough. Alan has really left. I guess he's too scared to face some of the difficulties we had. I assumed that everyone has the same desire as I have to solve their problems. I'm learning that's not so. The place feels empty now. I miss his sweetness and the security I got from being with someone.

"I'm questioning everything. I'm questioning if I'm in the right therapy and whether or not Anneliese is asking too much of me. Right now, I'm filled with doubts: about her, change, God, the works. I'm in a lot of pieces—I feel like the pieces of paint that got chipped off the phone in her waiting room when I slammed the phone down hard. I need help. I'm miserable. I've been crying steadily since he left. I know he was passive and sexually inadequate, but being so alone terrifies me. I'm in a million pieces. Help me pull them together."

Didi sobbed so deeply that she herself was astonished at the depth of her pain. Through her sobs, she suddenly realized that the sweetness and tenderness in which Alan had enveloped her should have been given by Rita. Because she had never been able to acknowledge the loss of her mother's tenderness, she too became contracted against her own warm feelings, seeking them elsewhere.

"I realize now that in return for his sweetness, I had to fill in for his limitations and his lopsidedness. This was okay for a while, but not forever. Since he was content to remain where we were, it was me who upset the apple cart. But how do I go on, saturated with so much despair?"

There was a brief silence after she had asked her question. Everyone spontaneously went to her. They held whatever parts of her body they could touch: her hands, arms, face, chest, even her legs and feet. She accepted this contact like an emotionally starved human being, which she was.

When one member looked into her eyes, Didi looked back as though for the first time. "Is this what it takes to be a human being? Do I have to go to the bottom of despair to be willing to let go of my defenses: the bravado and the arrogance?"

They nodded, remembering that their own despair had been a bottomless pit.

"Oh, how good it feels to be touched! Thank you! I wish I could take all of you home with me. How do I overcome this terrible loneliness? How do I live through it? It makes me feel suicidal. Alan was so unwilling to work on our relationship. That made me feel worthless and hurt me so much, I'm afraid I'll never be able to ask anyone for anything."

Richard, a member of the group, responded: "I've experienced what you're going through, Didi. I wanted to kill myself and almost succeeded because I could no longer bear the emptiness inside me. I couldn't fill it. I couldn't push it away. It remained around me like an octopus, strangling me with its tentacles. Losing my lover brought a tremendous amount of despair to the surface. I'm not a poet, but writing about my feelings while I was going through my hell helped me. Do you want to hear?"

Richard knew his poem by heart.

Alone—no one there.
Bobbing up and down in a
turbulent sea.
Treading water to stay afloat.

Arms too frenzied to reach.
Breath choking,
body stiff from keeping buoyant.

Throat contracted,
unable to scream,
to yell out to the vastness
for help.

Alone—
going my way?
The nipping of the
fish below.
The attack of sharks
that could send me
to a watery doom.

Fear—
only one way to go:
down,
down,
down,
an endless down.

Shall I wait for them
to accept me?
They never do!
They cannot,
they will not.

Why should they?
They received the same.

Shall I wait interminably,
knowing
it will never
happen?

No!
Pull up,
float on your back.
Look up at the sky.
Scream:
"Help me or I'll die.
Help me or I'll die."

The atmosphere resounds
with this plea.
Then,
silence everywhere.
An energy emerges—
faith is kindled—
a fusion with a vision.

A world of love and
understanding
fills me.
THEY are never too busy.
THEY pull me to their bosom.
I open to the heavenly sphere.
I feel supported,
wanted,
loved.

> This world will not
> betray me—
> EVER.

Didi listened intently. "But how do I arrive at such a place in myself?"

"Look within," advised Richard. Glancing toward me for permission, he suggested, "Let's do a meditation for inner guidance."

"Good idea, Richard," I said. "Didi, lie on the floor with the other members. Next to Richard, if you like."

I watched her settle beside him. She closed her eyes. I was astonished at how quickly she went into a meditative state. I sat next to her.

"I'm on the highest branch of a giant tree," said Didi after a while.

"Look down, Didi, to the place on the Earth from which you started your journey," I said.

"I'm so far away from the Earth," she answered. "I can barely remember I was on the ground just a few minutes ago."

"Go to the topmost branch and from there go to where your unconscious takes you," I whispered.

Didi laughed. "This is so nice. I've never wanted to be down there much. I tolerated it because I knew I had work to do. Oh, I like going up higher and higher and higher." She smiled with delight.

"What's happening, Didi?" I asked after a long silence.

"Miraculously large arms and hands are lifting me up. I'm getting lost in the ether. When I look down at the Earth, it's a pinpoint that's disappearing. Goodbye, Earth. I won't miss you. I'd rather be up here than down there. Oh, oh, I'm going up through layers and layers of mist. It's as though I'm going through an upended cornucopia, and hands and arms are pushing and pulling me through it until I come out of the top. Now, there's a large figure standing not too far away. I pull myself up farther.

"The figure beckons me to pull myself up still higher, to where it's standing. I scramble eagerly, arriving at its feet. I use every bit of energy to get there, but when I arrive, the figure pulls away from me and moves up farther so I have to make additional efforts to reach it. Finally it stands still and I find myself in front of it. When I look up at the figure, I see a huge angel. It has wings like angels are supposed to have.

"When I get accustomed to its size and beauty, I ask, 'Who are you?' It looks at me and answers, 'An ancient friend.'

"'What is your name?' I ask.

"'Simon.'"

Didi described him as a muscular, swarthy, male angel who said he had been with her for centuries. He told her that in her present life, although he had never gone away, he had, until this point, been shut out by her arrogance. He told her he was happy to be rediscovered and hoped they would have a lasting friendship.

Didi, in her trance state, said, "I look at him with my mouth agape. He's so familiar to me. I blink and blink to make sure that what is happening is real. I remember him from childhood. I used to call on someone when Rita was particularly vicious and there was no one else to turn to. I used to go to my room and look at the sky from my window and cry inwardly for someone to help me. I knew I couldn't cry out loud, because she would have come into my room, slapped me, and called me 'meshugana.'

"I remember that before he would make his presence known, there would be a humming or buzzing in my ears. I thought it was an insect around my head. But I never found an insect. Instead, the buzzing would get louder, until it felt like a dive bomber was crashing into my ears and going through my body. Even though I was only about seven or eight years old, the buzzing comforted me. I remember that after it stopped, I would feel enveloped in an indescribable warmth. That warmth created hope and confidence, and I wished to continue living. I knew I had a friend. 'Do you remember me when I was that young, Simon?'"

Simon assured Didi that he did remember, that he had comforted her until her teenage years. That was when Didi stopped listening, stopped tuning in, even though he had almost exploded her ear drums with his buzzing. Simon recalled that silently, in her spirit, Didi would yell at him, shouting that she could live her life by herself and that he wasn't needed. No actual words were exchanged, though, because the yelling and screaming occurred on a soul level. He recalled how she would ask what use he was when he couldn't change Rita's or Gary's behavior toward her.

No matter how often he explained that her parents were tests to be handled, she would assault him with her fury and reject him. One day Didi told him more emphatically than ever that she would no longer listen to him, that she would make her own decisions, and that he should stop buzzing around her ears. Simon said it was a significant time for both of them. At that point, he stopped contacting her, even though he continued to surround her with his energy.

Didi felt enriched as she spoke to her old friend. She wondered aloud how she could keep their communication alive. Simon advised her to keep growing and not get stuck in her defenses. He explained that her defenses thickened her energy field, making contact difficult. She promised to keep on her path, even though she was still reluctant to accept the idea that the arrogance and narcissism of her mother were aspects of her, too.

Didi bade farewell to Simon. "Thank you for being patient with me. I'll make every effort to stop creating barriers between us. Forgive me, Simon, for my trespasses."

"You are forgiven," Simon replied. "Look more closely into yourself and keep purifying and keep growing. I am always with you. Know this, and know that your connection to me as well as to our heavenly world is your true connection. Earth knowledge pales beside our heavenly wisdom. Your true Self will become steadily more available as your faith grows. Farewell, Didi. I am not far away. Call on me always."

Didi's closed eyes were filled with tears. I guided her down from the great height at which she had been communing with Simon, down to the tree, and back onto the earth.

When she was on the ground, she rubbed her eyes and exclaimed: "Oh, why do I have to come back here? It's so much nicer there!"

She paused, catching herself in a familiar disgruntled pattern. "I'm complaining again! And just now I made Simon a solemn promise to not create barriers. I'll keep that promise by staying in touch with his angelic energy. When I remember to do that, I feel so much better. I don't feel alone anymore. The despair diminishes. I feel hopeful and in touch with myself. I have energy to do what's next. I know I have to look at my arrogance. Can I wait until the next session, Anneliese, to do that? I have a lot to sort out from today's experience."

I agreed.

Didi thanked everyone for their warmth and understanding. Then she sat in amazement and awe as she listened to the members' higher-self experiences—much like the experience she'd had with Simon. Still buzzing from her contact with Simon and still in a somewhat heightened consciousness, Didi told everyone she saw the room populated by angels, who filled the space with love and joy.

Didi turned to me and said, "Forgive me for my doubts."

I told her that I feel doubts are an uncomfortable but necessary part of the growing process. Doubts, I said, as well as faith, are the rungs of the ladder upon which we tread. Doubts teach us the difference between losing our foothold and falling back, or stepping onto the next rung with faith and ascending.

"Good night, Didi," I said. "Good night, all."

Didi did not leave. She planted herself before me, wanting to tell me something. Her eyes were tearing. She, who was always talkative, was now mute. Her lips were moving but no sound came. I moved close to her. Finally I heard the words—

> I have a friend.
> His name is Simon.
> He is my angel
> who'll never leave.
> He's always loved me.
> I've never been alone.
> My life can be lived.

She looked into my face with so much love. No words came. She turned quickly and left.

33

Two of Didi's Past Lives

Didi rushed into the next session, breathless. She said that while she was riding on the subway to get to the session, she had been conversing with Simon with her eyes closed and had missed her stop. She was energized both from her dialogue with her angelic self and the physical effort of getting to my office. She told me how happy she was to have rediscovered Simon. She had contacted him every day since their reacquaintance.

I found Didi's transformation since the group session astonishing. I was once again convinced that when the higher self is available, the psyche is capable of handling any adversity. Alan was now in the past. Simon was a friend who understood her and gave her the confidence to face aspects of herself she had been unwilling to look at before. She was ready to search for an *arrogant, narcissistic, violent* woman, a woman whose qualities were not only Rita's but her own as well.

Didi lay on the bed ready for a regression, but also apprehensive. To ease her disquiet, I once again reminded her that the value of past-life information is to expand her consciousness, to give her a larger awareness of the complexity and multiplicity of her existence. I reminded her that when other lives became known to her, she would no longer remain trapped in a narrow, egocentric psyche, but would gain a more universal vision of the Self.

"I know. I know," said Didi. "But I'm still a little fearful about what I'll find, especially since I'm looking for a reflected version of my mother. Before I go there will you give me a hug?"

"I would be delighted to hug you," I said, and I did.

"That feels good. I'm ready."

I told her to breathe deeply, to increase her breathing until she became her breath.

"I'm dizzy," she said after a while. "I feel so light-headed. My body is spinning—spinning away from here."

She mumbled softly to herself. "There you are, Simon. Let me hold your hand." She lifted her right hand as though his hand were in hers. "I know you'll be with me as we go into the universe, back in time to when I was a woman like Rita—perhaps even a worse woman."

We're going into a deep darkness, to another time, another place, another me. We pass one shadow after another. I ask Simon if these shadows are lives of the past. He says they are, and that I'll stop in front of one that will show me a life giving me the information I need. He's let go of my hand, but I'm not afraid. I know he's still there. I'm very concentrated on what I'll discover. An image gradually grows clearer.

I'm a robust, dark-skinned Italian woman, walking before a servant who's pulling a wagon filled with terra cotta jugs. I see a well in the center of a small village. Women are gathered around it, filling their vessels with water. My servant will also fill our jugs with water when we arrive at the well.

From a distance I hear women gossiping and laughing good-naturedly. They like each other. I hear my name mentioned in hushed tones. They snicker and call me the town shrew. My servant smiles. I want to beat him. Instead, I walk along, seething. They joke about me, but they're afraid of my terrible temper. I feel powerful, knowing their fear of me.

We come closer to the well. I walk more determinedly into their midst, my eyes bulging with hatred. I stare down each one of them. I snort heavily, then spit in their faces. They wipe away my spit, quickly fill their jugs, place them on their heads, and hurry away toward the village and the houses where they live.

I order my servant to unload the jugs from the wagon and fill them with water. While he's doing so, I become aware of how lonely I am. I'd like to play and gossip with those women as they do with one another. I'd like to discuss my problems with them and get their sympathy. Instead, I'm always miserably alone, even though I have a husband.

My husband! Again I want to spit—spit a deadly poison that would maim him. My thoughts are loathsome, but I can't help myself. These thoughts overtake my brain and body, and I'm caught in their web like a dumb beast.

I notice my servant struggling with the jugs. They're made heavy by the precious water from the well. His foot slips on the wet cobblestones; one of the jugs falls to the ground, shattered. "Idiot! Idiot!" I scream. I grab an empty jug from the wagon and smash it on his head. He's stunned, bleeding. He reels, tries desperately to get his balance. I smirk at the sight of a man in pain and out of control. "We're losing time!" I shout. "Steady yourself, idiot!" I gruffly place my hands on his shoulders to steady him. He recovers, thanks me for my kindness, and apologizes for his awkwardness. I move away from him, wipe my contaminated hands on my skirt, all the while raging at having to put up with such a fool.

I walk ahead, my head held high in case a villager—any of the women—should see me. He pulls the heavy wagon with his struggling, bleeding body. I glimpse him from the corners of my eyes. What kind of subhuman have I become?

Lonely, lonely, unloved. I look in the direction of the village where the women live—with robust, vibrant men who greet them passionately. I fantasize that one of the men shouts to his woman, still a distance away, that she took too long to fill her jugs and that he wants to fill her with himself. He runs toward her, takes the jugs from her head, places them on the ground, pulls her onto his muscular body, lifts her into the air until both of them squeal with delight. I envision him letting her down, pressing his hot, erect penis against her vagina while their lips meet and their tongues passionately seek the other's. They get a foretaste of a greater pleasure. They're unable to tear themselves apart.

He carries her to a grassy, hidden spot underneath a tree by their house. In this place, he ravages her, takes her into his longing arms as he licks her, bites her, squeezes his body into hers. Their genitals join as they moan and groan in ecstasy. This union needs no words. They're joined for good, with excitement, passion, and pleasure. From their lovemaking come their children. They live their lives without regret.

"I want this! I want it all! I dream of making love with someone like that! Why can't I have it, too? Oh, God! I want this closeness! I must have it or I'll die."

These are the feelings inside me as I walk along the dusty road to my home, my body shuddering with desire. I can't let any of these emotions be seen, however. Instead, I stiffen my body against them, and while I'm doing so I experience a fleeting moment of clarity.

Most weak, passive men, my feeble servant included, can't match my passionate nature. This kind of man is all too familiar to me. I grew up with a father who was such a man, I'm going home to such a man, and I want to smash such weak, passive men to bits. The more I think about men like that, the more enraged I become. I froth with fury that the servant can't pull the wagon with brute, male strength. The wagon represents me. I become obsessed with the idea that my womanhood is not being met. I turn around and scream at him. "Hurry up, you scum, we don't have all day! If you can't do the job properly, I'll get someone who can!"

We arrive home. I set my jaw and raise my head high. I'm emotionally invulnerable. My servant pulls the wagon into the courtyard and unloads the jugs. Every heavy jug he lifts from the wagon brings forth a heart-wrenching groan of pain that he tries to stifle by pretending to clear his throat.

His groans call my husband's attention. He peers into the courtyard from behind a curtained window. The curtains are quickly pushed into place. This is unusual for him. "Is he coming out to greet me?" My fantasy gets ignited. "Will he sweep me into his muscular arms?" I wait breathlessly, hoping to be enveloped in a loving embrace. "No! No! Always no!" He rushes past me in the direction of my servant, then scowls back at me as he lifts the servant's almost comatose body off the ground and carries him to his quarters. He mutters under his breath, "You did it again! Violent, selfish woman!"

I stand dazed. My shattered hopes become like a still, stiff death. I lift my head defiantly, lift my skirt a few inches off the ground, and stomp into the house.

In the privacy of our bedroom I undress, wash my hardened, robust body, and sigh, sigh without ceasing, until tears come to my eyes. *I'm astonished that I'm crying. I cry, cry, cry until my tear ducts are dry. I remember it was thirty years ago when I had shed my last tears.*

Didi became quiet. "I'm so sad," she moaned. "So sad. Simon, where are you?" She held her hand out in the air. "I need you. Why am I so sad?"

"I'm here, Didi! I told you I would help you! Look deeply into the shadow. Let yourself fall into it and you will get the answer you are looking for," Simon assured her.

"I'm falling into it. It's as though I'm twirling and twirling right into the center of it, and when I'm in the center, I stop twirling. Everything stops. I see a little girl of four in a kitchen. She's crying in total anguish. Something has happened to her."

My chest, oh, my chest!
"Mommy! Daddy!
It hurts. Oh, it hurts."

Scalding water, a
greasy white cloth
on my chest. Oh,
the pain! The pain!

"You were under my
feet, always around,
naughty child, always
around."

Such is my mother.
My father looks on,
fearful of her—
always fearful.

I faint from my pain.
They fetch a doctor.
He has kind, green eyes.
His hands heal my
scalded skin.
He must be God.

My chest becomes
scarred.
She insists I do
chores.
Too soon—
the scars become
infected.
She'll not let me
rest.
My chest becomes
deformed.
Serves you right,
little girl.
You were always
around.

I grow to be a woman
of twenty-one.
I had no suitors.
My mother rebukes
me.
"You'll be an ugly
old maid."

A young lad
fancies me.
I suggest we marry.

*He knows of my dowry
and promptly consents.*

*My parents are shocked—
she, that someone wants
me—
he, shocked and terrified—
the household would now
become his sole hell.*

*They give us a wedding.
I'm ecstatic to leave them,
to start life anew—
a life with some
happiness.*

*Our wedding night is
a fiasco.
I undress before him.
He sees my deformity.
He turns away.
The sexual act is perfunctory.
I remain empty, forlorn,
hopeless about life.*

*I gradually become cruel,
vicious,
impossible to be around.
I'm a shrew like my
mother.*

*My husband and I
stick together.
He'll not give up*

> *the dowry.*
> *I feel like a freak.*
> *"Who else would want me?"*
>
> *"I want to die, to die—*
> *but would they accept*
> *me in heaven?*
> *God! God!*
> *Why such a miserable*
> *life?*
> *Why?*
> *What have You to say*
> *about a life*
> *without a shred*
> *of love in it?"*

Didi was still involved in her story. From her body language, I surmised that she, as the character, was dying—dying because she wanted to. Her husband was by her side. Her breath stopped. She left that life hearing him repeat, "What a waste. What a waste." She remembered these words as she climbed into a mist referred to by mystics as the *bardo*, the state after death.

"What's happening now, Didi?"

"I'm walking through grassy fields. I'm alone. I don't want to call on Simon, because I don't want to misuse his kindness. I'm so nervous. I know I'll have to answer for the life I just had. I'd better get on with it.

"I come to a large table under a big tree. A lot of figures, all in white, sit around this table. Everything is so familiar. I have the feeling I've been here many, many times before. I can't help it, but when I talk to them, I'm filled with arrogance."

"What do you say?"

"'I know what You're all thinking.'

"It's not a horrible statement, but I say it with a very specific attitude. The arrogance is unmistakable.

"A beautiful woman answers, 'Yes, Didi, your arrogance is still present.' She beckons me to sit with Them. I suddenly feel transparent. I feel as though my sensibilities become like Theirs. I'm so ashamed. I lower my head as I realize I came into that life loaded with anger and misery. Anger because I didn't want to be there. Misery because I hated every aspect of living. 'Why me?' was a question I always had in my mind. I was determined to be a victim, which perversely fueled my arrogance and brutishness."

"Are they aware of what you're feeling? There doesn't seem to be an exchange of words. Is it like telepathic communication?" I asked, curious about how she was getting her information.

"It's like being at the height of your sensitivity with someone, and you really don't have to use words. It's kind of wonderful, because interaction has a distinct, intuitional rhythm."

"What are you feeling now, Didi—now that you have become aware of your unwillingness to be on the Earth?"

"I'm deeply ashamed. I feel guilt for my transgressions against life, living, and God. Being aware is one thing, though. Changing it is another."

Didi stopped speaking. She was completely absorbed with the heavenly entities. I watched her facial expressions as well as her body language. There was an intensity in her breathing. She suddenly raised her right hand, her index finger pointed toward someone. Her face was contorted with anger. I urged her to speak out loud, to share with me what was happening.

She yelled, "So, when are You going to make me Your special angel? What do You mean, I'm not ready? There's always more to learn and understand? What kind of cockamamie answer is that?"

She then thrust both arms into the air as though she were trying to hold onto God, Himself, tugging at Him, trying to fasten herself to Him. She yelled louder than I had ever heard her yell, "*I want to be an angel. I could be a good angel. Who do You think You are, telling me I wouldn't be a good angel? If I have to go down again, You'll be sorry! Very sorry!*"

Didi sobbed and sobbed. In between her sobs, she told me she had been shown the initial layer, where it had all begun, where she had been a particle of protoplasm, a soul nestled in the firmament. It was there her rage at God had been initiated, when He had ordered her out of His kingdom, when her many descents to Earth began, and when rectification and redemption to gain a truer Self had become the purpose of her soul's incarnations.

"Didi, would you like to come down to Earth now? You might have had enough probing for today?"

She shook her head violently. "I can't leave now. I wouldn't be able to live with myself. I was a horrible woman in that last life, certainly a replication of my mother in this life. I was arrogant and demanding with God. I did everything wrong. There has to be another life where I'm a better person. I want to go back up there and be shown another life, maybe that of a man. I was a horrendous woman. Maybe, just maybe, I might have some redeeming qualities as a male, even though the qualities we've discovered are *passive, self-indulgent, arrogant*."

"Okay," I began. "Make yourself ready. Breathe deeply, with your mouth open. Envision yourself going to the large table around which the Sages sit. Breathe deeply until you find yourself in front of them. Tell them how unhappy you are, how you want to find a male life, a life that might redeem the female life you just discovered."

"I'm there. I'm telling them. They consent. They open a large book. They tell me it's the Akashic record, which contains the history of every human being in the entire universe. I look on expectantly. I ask timidly if perhaps it might be a better life than the previous one. They smile but say nothing.

"They tell me to look into the pages with my name on the top. I look and look. It's as though I'm getting pulled into the pages, and I begin to feel dizzy. I'm mesmerized by the pages and have no control of my own. When they see me in this state, they invite me to sit beside them. I do. Close to them, I find that their emanation makes me spin inwardly and outwardly, faster and faster, away from the table around which we're sitting, to a distant, distant dark place."

*Dark, huge brute of a man
on a battlefield.
I think I'm Napoleon.
I strut and gesture,
forgetting who
I really am—
an officer,
second in
command.*

*My men are disgusted
by my posturing,
but don't dare show
their contempt.
Instead they applaud me
as I parade before them.
This makes me feel
I'm someone.*

*A young recruit,
not knowing of
my megalomania,
turns his back to
unbuckle his sword.
I see his back.
I become apoplectic
with rage.
I go to him,
lift him bodily
into the air.
I place his head
and neck tightly
under my arm.*

*He's in a noose,
fighting like a
captured animal.*

*I strut around the
battlefield, the
recruit choking.
I gesticulate wildly
with my other arm,
while I tell the men
of my heroic exploits
during our warfare.
At the same time,
the recruit struggles
desperately in my
fierce grip,
as I
expostulate
endlessly.*

*The men in the
battalion applaud
my drama.
They do so hoping
I'll stop.
If I persist,
they fear
the recruit will choke
to death.
They applaud more
wildly,
hoping I'll let go
of him.*

*Satisfaction runs
through me—
their applause
appeases.
I let go of the
recruit
whose gasps are
near-death
rattlings.
I go to my quarters
feeling greater—
much greater
than
Napoleon.*

"More arrogance, more self-indulgence, more of everything that's horrible. So what else is new? So why should I rectify? What's redeeming about me? *Nothing!*"

Didi was in total despair. She resorted to her arrogance. "I thought you would give me a redeeming male life. You're cruel! You're just socking it to me!"

She told me the Sages were waiting for her to look at Them, but she turned her head away. She would have stayed in that position interminably had not a Sage whom she sensed as playful come from the table to stand directly in front of her. She turned her head to the other side. When the Sage moved to stand in front of her, she burst into laughter despite her painful state. She looked at Him quizzically. "This game is familiar, but I don't know when I played it. Maybe when I was a child?" The Sage beckoned her to look ahead of her, into the mist.

"I see a strange contraption. It looks like a silvery net with a long pole attached to it. I'm in it. I'm not alone. A huge angel sits in front of me, but I'm furious and won't look at him. He jumps around, trying to get my attention. He looks as though he's doing a jig as he hops from one side to the other. This makes us both laugh. The angel then becomes clearer."

Didi was silent for a long time. I saw her face twist into disbelief at what she was realizing. She screamed: "You're doing the same jig now as you did in the contraption. You're the Angel of Destiny! It's you who took me down there! It's you who caught me and shoved me into that woman's womb. I could kill you for betraying me! Why did you do it?" Didi lay on the bed, her arms folded, her face in a contorted fury, her body stiff and breathless.

She lay in this stiffness until I asked her what was happening to her. "I sit immobilized for a long time. Again, I would have stayed furious forever. Instead, I'm suddenly inundated with insights. I become sharply aware of how monumental my resistance is to being on Earth and to rectifying my problems. I become aware of how I've gone through this life and others, avoiding all truths about myself."

Didi felt devastated. "What a coward I've been—never wanting to face life or myself. How much life and energy I've wasted. How abusive I've been to others."

I tried to console her. "We are all victims and victimizers until the chain is broken."

"And how does it get broken?" she asked forlornly.

"Do you want to continue, Didi?" I asked, concerned that she might be overloaded.

"I've got to go on. I can't stop now."

She was again quiet.

"What's happening?"

"I'm still with the Sages. I'm enveloped in light. They're focused on me. Simon stands beside me. I hold his hand. He's so consoling. I tell him that I love him. He smiles. The light becomes brighter and then shapes become visible. Oh, no! I'm back on the battlefield. The maniacal soldier appears with the recruit's head underneath his arm. Then everything gets blurred. Suddenly the light gets clearer. Now the soldier and the recruit change into other forms. Oh, no! I can't believe this. The soldier becomes *me* and the recruit *my mother*!

"I shout to the Sages. 'No! Disgusting! Don't play games with me! She was a horrible mother!' I'm furious. 'You're telling me that her behavior in this life is retribution for what I did to her when she was the recruit?'"

Didi banged her fists on the bed, screaming, "No! No! No! I won't accept this. It's crazy. You're all crazy!"

She continued, "The Sages wait for my fury to subside. Simon's patience and love for me placate my wrath. He holds my hands as he tells me that I've come into their midst to learn. 'Don't resist what they're revealing. Look closely, learn and grow.'

"'I'll try.'"

Didi recovers from her fury. She tells me that the Sages are communicating with her. There are no words, just thought forms. "I slowly begin to understand that Rita's behavior in this life is overblown, that as a child, the punishment I got from her was always excessive for the misdemeanors I committed. I never understood before why she was always so cruel, so much in a rage toward me. Now I understand why.

"Simon explains that humans act from multidimensional, unconscious facets in their psyches. These facets might be expressed toward others in the most bizarre, inexplicable ways.

"I listen to their explanations with wonder. The Sages are pleased that I'm finally receptive. I marvel at the complexity of our existence. I no longer feel the need to rave and rant. But where did it all begin?

"'Look into the mist,' says Simon.

"Again I see myself as a blob of protoplasm in the firmament. I follow God everywhere. I'm like His shadow. I want to be His special angel. My rage is boundless when I'm told I'm not ready. Again I leave the firmament blaspheming, hating, abusing. Because I insist on being like God, I create havoc on Earth. The guilt I refuse to feel rigidifies inside me as arrogance. Arrogance makes me feel that I'm somebody."

Simon tells her that in a state of arrogance, she creates more arrogance and consequently more guilt. Living becomes an endless circle of distortion.

"When does it end? What must I do to break it? These lives make me feel hopeless, that I'm not worth helping. Isn't there one life where I did something right, when I wasn't abusive? If not, then cast me into the depths of hell, where I'll learn what I need to know or disappear into the bowels of the Earth and live forever like a beast."

I interrupted, "You've gone through enough. Come down, say goodbye to Simon and the Sages. Thank Them for Their help."

She opened her eyes. She was forlorn and despairing.

"Didi, understand that living our lives is like balancing a scale. Sometimes lives tip toward malevolence; at other times, toward righteousness. Your soul calls upon the psyche to rectify misdeeds, and when choices are made, the balance of the scale changes. The aim of rectification is to have fewer and fewer gaps between the malevolent and the righteous forces in us. Processing our guilt and our choices through an ever-growing, enlightened consciousness enables the scale to come to equilibrium.

"You feel bogged down right now, thinking that arrogance, narcissism, and violent behavior are your only qualities. That's not so. I personally find you to be generous, wise, energetic, insightful. You've been good to me and to others.

"Know that you've been searching for a truer self since you were nineteen. Your soul is urging you to deepen that search. That's why you are here. A person with less soul-prompting would not know there is 'more, more of Self.' In our next session," I concluded, "let's look for a life of fullness and richness, just to give you the experience that the scale can tip the other way. Okay?"

"Okay! I feel better now. This is powerful stuff. It's not nice stuff, but I've got to face it. If nothing else comes from what I've gone through today, I'm deeply certain that I want to face it. You'll be available if I need you, Anneliese?"

"I'll be a phone call away, Didi."

She gave me a weary but hopeful hug. I held her strongly.

34

Another Life with a Pinch of Arrogance

When Didi next entered my office, I noticed a change. I often recognize a difference in the facial expressions of people who go through a transformation. It has been said that pain makes one beautiful. Pain often brings one to the core of the Self and the Self, in its splendid honesty, is always beautiful.

Didi sat in her chair as usual, but instead of perching on the edge of her seat, she sat back in the chair and waited for me to speak. I looked at her angelic face. I asked her if it had been a difficult week.

She told me that she had been in a lot of pain, but after several days, the understanding she had acquired from the last session took hold and made her feel clearer.

"Because I understood that we humans interact with one another repeatedly, switching roles constantly, I was able to look at my mother differently. I realized that one of us has to stop the battle that's gone on between us for centuries. Since she's unaware, it had to be me. So, I called her during the week and showed some concern about her health, which she'd been complaining about. I can't say that I'm filled with genuine, good feelings toward her but what's important is that I'm not perpetuating bad feelings."

"What was her response to your change of attitude?"

Didi shrugged her shoulders, telling me that Rita had been a little shocked, but had liked it. "She likes it because she's become more humble and more genuinely open since my father's death.

"Despite her humility, though, Rita managed to flare up from time to time while we were talking. What's new and different is that I wasn't reactive. I just told her what I was feeling with as much honesty as was available to me. I was surprised that my new attitude seemed to take away her need to go into a tirade. Had I not experienced the past life of the soldier, I would have continued fighting her to the end of our lives.

"This was a gargantuan feat for me. But even so, I'm sad. Reflectivism took me out of my victimization, but where am I? I need a shot of positive energy—another life which will inspire me to recognize qualities that are good, strong, loving—qualities that make me feel good about myself, that will inspire me to long for and search deeply for the intrinsic Didi."

"You're right, Didi," I affirmed. "Every human being needs to get a glimpse of the real Self. Let's look for her. Lie on the bed. Make yourself available for the beauty in you."

Didi's eyes shone. She felt hopeful. She breathed deeply throughout her body, more deeply than at any other time. She was filled with enthusiasm. She told me she believed she would be a woman. "Simon, wherever You are, show me the real me. I need to be in touch with me more than ever in my life. Show her to me. I know she's in me. Let me see her, get close to her, know her heart. Simon, please help me."

She listened for His voice. Before long, she heard Him say: "Trust your heart and what it says to you, Didi. Feel its rhythm. Let it give you another image from which to see yourself. Feel this image and clarify it."

"She's young," Didi began. "About thirteen, blond, red-cheeked, alive, strong, healthy, happy. She's in a family of five children in medieval times. My parents are English aristocrats, who love their children. There's always excitement in our home. Music, love, storytelling, and learning are daily events."

I love to learn,
to ride horses,
to climb trees.
Energy, energy,
I'm filled with it.
My parents love me
and I love
them and all my
siblings.

Laughter, excitement,
and joy fill our home.
I cannot get enough
of life.

One day many men
come to our manor.
Relatives from another
village.
Backslapping, hugs,
laughter, gossip.
I'm transfixed
by so many strangers.

Among them is a
handsome young man,
five years
older than me.
We shake hands.
I feel shy,
I look toward the
ground.
But somehow I know
he'll be my husband.

They stay three days.
I learn about births,
weddings, death of kin.
I hear about feuds,
of bloodshed and warring
lords.
When it is time for them
to leave,
I burst into
tears.
Everyone knows it's because
of the young man.

He comes to me.
He holds my hands.
He looks into my eyes.
He vows to return.
I smile with joy.
We know we'll be
betrothed when
I reach fifteen.

At fifteen, my beloved
comes to our house.
He asks my father
for my hand in
marriage.
My father consents,
beaming with delight,
as does my mother
when she is told.

My suitor then
approaches me,
his soon-to-be wife.

*I take him to my
favorite tree.
I climb to the highest
branch.
He follows, sitting
opposite me.*

*He proposes,
looking into my
beaming face.
I climb down,
waiting
for him to follow.*

*When we're on the ground,
He takes me in his
arms and kisses me
with heart-filled love.*

*I restrain our passion,
for we are not yet wed.
We enter my home,
where congratulations
are given.
My family rejoices
with singing, laughter,
and heavenly music.
God, Your presence
is felt.*

*The time arrives
to leave my home,
after packing all my
belongings.
My family, my love,*

*and I
journey to his
village,
where the wedding
takes place—
a joyous event
lasting a week.*

*When the guests
have left,
we love each other
passionately.
His manhood is
strong and tenderly
expressed.
I feel
no one could be
happier
than
we.*

*We have three children,
who are loved as we
were.
They grow up and
eventually leave us.
We have grandchildren
when I reach forty.
Our lives are blessed.*

*At forty-five feuds
spring up around us.
The atmosphere becomes
dark and foreboding.
My husband prepares*

> *our home for a siege.*
> *The fighting begins,*
> *with me at his side.*
>
> *I shoot arrows at*
> *the invaders.*
> *When I'm not shooting*
> *I prepare the weapons,*
> *readying them for my*
> *husband's use.*
> *I'm fearless but careless.*
> *I expose my body*
> *while aiming at an*
> *enemy.*
> *An arrow enters my*
> *heart.*
> *I fall backward—*
> *dead.*
>
> *My husband tries*
> *to dislodge the arrow,*
> *tugging at it with*
> *cries of anguish.*
> *He cannot dislodge it.*
> *His pain turns to rage.*
> *He kills the man who*
> *brought death to his*
> *wife.*

Didi, lying on the bed, kept tugging at the arrow in her chest. She screamed: "I don't want to die yet! It's such a good life! Do something! Get the arrow out of my chest! I don't want to leave you!" Rolling from side to side, she tugged and pulled at the imaginary arrow, hoping to dislodge it.

I urged her to acknowledge her death, but she resisted, though finally she let go and went to the *bardo*.

"Once again I'm standing unhappily before the large table occupied by the beatific Sages. I'm furious. 'Who decided to tear me out of that life? I demand to see God!'

"'You will,' They answer. 'First, let's discuss this last life and what you learned from it.'

"'What do You mean—what I learned from it? You want a report now in the midst of my pain?'"

Didi, in the presence of the Sages, becomes aware of her arrogant attitude. She changes it and is more real, weeping softly as she tells Them how unhappy she is to leave that life. She tells them how much she loved her husband and her children and how satisfying that love was. "I'm capable of sweetness, kindness, and selflessness. I felt whole. I was such a good woman. I learned I can be true to myself and be accepted for it. And now it's over before it should be."

Didi pleads with them to be sent back to complete that life. She rationalizes that she needed more time to cherish those aspects of her nature.

The Sages try to console her. Simon tries to console her. He explains that she should realize this life was a gift, which she should be grateful for and learn from. He tells her, "This life has given you a glimpse of your capabilities and God's love. Destiny gives exactly what the psyche can handle. Even though you believe you can handle more, you must trust Our decision. In your case, the scale is not yet sufficiently tipped toward righteous living. Your unwieldy unconscious cannot yet be trusted not to betray your Self. You will have to live many more lives to grow your way into fuller consciousness.

"The temptation is to forget the unsavory aspects of your nature, minimize them, and live as though you had truly earned redemption. This will surely fatten your arrogance and keep you from seeing or struggling with your rage at God. Destiny is wiser than we know and the scales come to equilibrium only when redemption is earned."

"What do you feel about what Simon is saying, Didi?" I asked.

"I open my mouth to argue with Him, but no words come. I open my heart instead. But, I can't let go of my disappointment at God.

"They postpone my next incarnation indefinitely, until I can more readily absorb the teachings of the Sages. My rage at God gradually diminishes. My arrogance also diminishes. I fight with these forces all the time. It's a battle I'm determined to win. I know that one day I'll be victorious. In the meantime, my struggle continues unceasingly."

Didi returned to consciousness, shaking her head. "It takes so long to be purged of such an ancient, embedded, unconscious rage at God. It was easier with Rita. Nevertheless, freeing myself from that rage at God will mean becoming free of the last shred of victimization.

"I learned from the last life that I have beautiful qualities. They're a part of me. I must remember them and ask each day for divine guidance and for help in realizing who I truly am. Most important, I must ask for extra-special help in dropping my case against God."

I said, "If you drop your case against God, Didi, your soul will sing."

Didi smiled. She understood that she understood. She realized she had a lot of work to do, but contrary to what was going on with her when she first began her sessions with me, she was now willing to do it with a more expanded consciousness.

She no longer perched on the edge of her seat like a needy, devouring child. Instead she sat with her feet on the ground, energized in her body, in touch with her angelic Self. She said, quietly:

> My wrath is going.
> I'm rectifying
> and being redeemed.
>
> I step on my rung
> of the ladder
> and—
> look
> up.

Guide to Terms Used in This Book

Bioenergetics. "A therapeutic technique to help a person get back together with his body and to help him enjoy to the fullest degree possible the life of the body. This emphasis on the body includes sexuality . . . as well as breathing, moving, feeling and self-expression." (*Bioenergetics*, Alexander Lowen, M.D., p. 43, Coward, McCann & Geoghegan, Inc., NY 1975.) This therapeutic modality was founded by Dr. Alexander Lowen and Dr. John Pierrakos.

Breathing Stool. A therapeutic tool devised by Drs. Lowen and Pierrakos to help the patient elicit breathing. It is two feet in height. Rolled blankets secured by cords are placed on it. The patient arches face-up over the stool, feet grounded under the legs. This stress position will elicit breathing. The patient's capacity or incapacity to breathe gives the therapist information about the "armoring" of the patient's body.

Armoring. A term coined by Wilhelm Reich, founder of Vegetotherapy, the root of Bioenergetics. Armoring refers to the muscular tension in the body that provides a shield against painful and threatening emotional experiences. The organism can begin its armoring from the time of birth, if not before.

Use of Tennis Racket. The racket is held in both hands and the arms are stretched behind the shoulders, head, and body. The body is thus in an arched position, coming from grounded legs and feet. When it is in this position for a period of time, breathing is elicited, particularly when the mouth is ajar. The entire body becomes activated. The racket is used to hit a bed that is customarily present in the therapist's office for this purpose.

Hitting the bed from this arched position is used to express the rage the person is contending with.

Symbiosis. The paralyzed emotional state of two people who cannot separate themselves from each other because they have pasted images of their parents onto the other. In such a state, neither person lives from himself/herself. This superimposed state serves to keep the psyche alive, since living through another gives the person an identity.

Reflectivism. The belief that in a noncoincidental universe, qualities from your past existences purposefully occur in your parents, to be "reflected" once more in you. By being the object of actions you once imposed upon others, you can face, accept, and surmount your own limitations. It is a concept of self-responsibility and self-absolution.

Discovering the Male Energy (right side of the body). Start from a grounded position. Stretch the right arm, starting from the fingers of the right hand, until the stretch goes into the right side of the body. When this side is stretched to its ultimate capacity, the body will naturally fall into a particular position. Bring your consciousness to that position, feel the content of that position, express from that content. Continue from that position to another and another, until the male side speaks clearly and distinctly about itself.

Discovering the Female Energy (left side of the body). Do with the left side what was done with the right side. The final result is that the female energy will speak clearly and distinctly about itself.

ALSO FROM ANT HILL PRESS...

Soul Play: Turning Your Daily Dramas into Divine Comedies
Vivian King, Ph.D.

"Who would have thought a self-help book could be so much fun and so profoundly impactful at the same time. I highly recommend *Soul Play* to those committed to taking charge of their lives."
Jack Canfield
Co-author, *Chicken Soup for the Soul*

"*Soul Play* presents an entertaining and effective way to discover, develop, and integrate the many archetypal energies that exist within us all."
Shakti Gawain
Author, *Creative Visualization* and *Living in the Light*

○ ○ ○

My Female, My Male, My Self, and God:
A Modern Woman in Search of Her Soul
Anneliese Widman, Ph.D.

"Anneliese Widman, a well-known New York psychotherapist, has given us an unusual and poetic spiritual autobiography. Her book will be an inspiration to all those who have struggled with the scars of early abuse and its attendant pain and confusion in adult life and relationship. As she movingly documents, it is only by patient reflection on the deeper spiritual meaning in our suffering and by finding a full and honest relationship with ourselves—both the dark and the light within us—that we can find peace and wholeness. A fine, courageous, and challenging book."
Roger J. Woolger, Ph.D.
Author, *Other Lives, Other Selves* and *The Goddess Within*